INVESTED
Prayers

MARGARET A. MEARS
AND HARVEY MEARS

ISBN 978-1-63903-644-8 (paperback)
ISBN 978-1-63903-645-5 (digital)

Copyright © 2021 by Margaret A. Mears and Harvey Mears

All rights reserved. No part of this publication may be reproduced, distributed, or transmitted in any form or by any means, including photocopying, recording, or other electronic or mechanical methods without the prior written permission of the publisher. For permission requests, solicit the publisher via the address below.

Christian Faith Publishing, Inc.
832 Park Avenue
Meadville, PA 16335
www.christianfaithpublishing.com

Printed in the United States of America

Introduction

Everyone has a story, and most Christians have a testimony. This book contains a collection of testimonies accompanied with memoirs from the authors. It is very important for God's people to go and witness to the unsaved, to the lost and confused, and to all those living in darkness. The testimonies contain actual experiences or messages. The testimonies express the praises of God. Most of the testimonies are manifestations of invested prayers. The authors coined the phrase "invested prayers" from observing the discussions stemming from memoirs on given topics. We observed that repeatedly making references to manifestations in our lives were the results of prayers we had prayed and the prayers others have prayed on our behalf.

History will have us believe that slaves invested prayers for their freedom. We believe Nelson Mandela invested prayers for his freedom. Some cancer survivors invested prayers for their healing. Some prisoners invested prayers or had loved ones invest prayers for redemption and freedom. We believe prayers were invested for the atheists, gangbangers, and wayward children would be converted to choosing a better lifestyle. To invest in prayers is to communicate with God our request or requests. We are encouraged to believe God will answer prayer; yet we have to remember that prayers are answered in God's time, not our time.

Every testimony was given and received for God to receive the glory. The responses were given in reflections of past individual experiences as related to each testimony shared. This book was primarily written to tell the story of a former drug addict and the mishaps and sins of a backsliding mother and wife. The purpose is to share how God delivers, heals, provides, restores, and comforts us. God converts wrong thinking to better thinking and decision making. It's no secret what God can do. Prayer investors have expressed seeing Jesus as a way maker, as a promise keeper, a miracle worker, and as a light in the darkness.

God Is Real

Margaret's Story

I was born in a small section of Baltimore called Cherry Hill. My parents were Annie and Sweeney Boone. The family grew to four children to include Donald, David, and Mildred. We were a modest living family. There were times my mother had to borrow because the money my father sent didn't arrive in the mail in time to meet the essentials. My father was a merchant seaman. He was sailing more than he was home. We had two grandmothers to help us financially. I loved school, and I loved going to church. Mother suffered from asthma almost daily. We lived in the projects for four years, then we moved to Gwynn Avenue. As the first Black family to move on that block, we were faced with uncomfortable living conditions, confronting racism. We were not welcomed. Windows were broken with rocks, threats were made, and the police had to guard our house for three weeks. I am grateful that I had enough by Sunday school training to avoid prejudiced attitudes. I love people despite their ethnocentrism. I remember my mother in her ailing condition, standing firm and investing prayers for our security. I developed a phobia of dogs when my brother and I were chased to school by boys holding barking dogs. Let God arise and my enemies be gathered.

    I was just slightly above average in school. I allowed physical insecurities to hold me back from excelling to my full potential. I made the mistake in elementary school of comparing myself to other classmates. The outcome resulted in me thinking light-skinned classmates had better hair and appearances, and I was dark-skinned with skinny legs and nappy hair. I struggled to feel good enough or feel accepted. Thank God I overcame those negative thoughts. I learned to believe and receive; Jesus loves me. I came so close to missing my high school graduation due to a hemorrhaging menstrual cycle. I was very weak. I had to walk almost sideways along the Civic Center wall in fear of falling or fainting. I made it, and six decades later, I remember the smile on my mother's face when I walked across the stage to receive my diploma. She had passed away when I graduated from Coppin State College with my bachelor of science degree, but I felt her presence through the Spirit. I always knew I wanted to be a teacher, and God allowed me to achieve that goal. Praise God from whom all blessings flow.

I was married to Robert Woods at the age of twenty-six. He lived in Brooklyn, New York, and I lived in Baltimore. For two months I commuted on weekends until Robert firmly said I had to move permanently. He had his own home, his own car, and a real decent job. He met all my criteria for a good husband. We adopted my precious daughter, Erica. Our marriage could be described as being on a roller coaster. We loved each other, and Erica was the binding force. Robert was previously married, no children. His divorce came through three days before our wedding. I was really fearful. I had planned a big wedding with twelve bridesmaids and twelve groomsmen. My brother, Donald, was best man and Cynthia Ford was my maid of honor. The wedding was great. Despite the numerous separations, we remained married for thirty years and five months. Robert passed on April 26, 2004. I have so many memories from this marriage.

I have so many memories of deaths in our family. I have numerous memories relating to my career as a special education teacher. Regrettably, I have memories of my extramarital adventure and other backsliding behavior. But God saw the best in me and allowed me to repent. I am pressing on.

I was a widow for ten years, and this period of life brought me closer to the Lord. God heard my invested prayers and sent me a husband I adore, Harvey Mears. The story goes on.

Sometimes I Feel Like a Motherless Child

Harvey's Story

My story, my testimony started on my ninth birthday, which I shared with my twin brother and two sisters; our mother passed away. Although we were very sad, we didn't fully understand death. For months I believed what my grandmother told us that my mother went to heaven and she would return. I received spanking after spanking for gazing in the sky, waiting for my mother to come down from the sky. My grandmother took on the responsibilities of keeping the four of us together. She raised us because other relatives wanted to pick, choose, or separate us. Grandma, Helen Mears, made us attend church services every Sunday and Wednesday. We had to memorize scriptures from the Bible and recite them once a week at home before Sunday morning breakfast. We frequently witnessed grandma praying and worshipping God. Bottom line: we knew right from wrong. We were taught to work hard. Respect and good manners were not an option; we had to demonstrate these behaviors at home, in school, in church, and in our neighborhood.

As we grew older, I became curious about the fun my friends and neighbors were experiencing while we were in the house, garden, yard, or anywhere my stern grandmother wanted us to work. Grandma was very sweet, but she didn't play. She didn't spare the rod. I wish I had a dollar for every whooping I received; I even received whoopings to cover or prevent my siblings from receiving a whooping they rightfully deserved. I have no regrets about those incidents because it was done and received in love. I know Grandma loved me. I know Jesus loves me.

I was born with an odd-shaped head. During my school years, I was constantly teased about the shape of my head. My head was described by too many classmates, so-called friends, and even some relatives as a "football head," "long head," or "hatch head." These names offended me deeply, and I started responding with my fist in brutal fights and cruel cursing. Those vengeful responses didn't stop the tears I shed secretly or the foundation of hate that was building in my heart. I suffered with pains of bitterness, especially after my mother died. As time went on, I hated to hear boys talk about their mothers. I was jealous because my mother was dead. I couldn't go home and tell anyone about the unfair experiences.

When I shared those horrible incidents with Grandma, she told me to ignore the offenders. One spring day, she took me outside to her flower garden and asked me, "What do you see?" I told her I saw flowers; then she pointed out the differences in the flowers to let me know that God made everybody differently. After this lesson, I discovered that wearing a hat or a cap made the shape of my head less noticeable. The fights also decreased, but the bitterness lingered. The cursing and threatening warnings from my mouth increased. Yes, I could cut you down with my verbal response in a second. My fighting reputation, my physical size, and my big mouth were my new weapons. The older I got, the more intense and more habitual my new responses grew.

My story includes incarnations, resentments, relationships, and recovery. I can truly say that the Lord has brought me from a mighty long way. I have come up on the rough side of the mountain, but through it all, God had his hands on me. You will receive more details of my story as I reacted and made associations to the various testimonies. My motive for revealing my story is to convey to anyone, especially the addict, that with God, all things are possible. We have the resources to direct us, to teach us, and to guide us in all of our endeavors and challenges in life. I am proclaiming salvation from Jesus, God's mercies, and the acceptance of the Holy Spirit. I am far from perfect, but now I see myself as God sees me, an incomplete work in the process.

Invested Prayers

Larry Cypress

When I was seven years old, I received a whooping from my mother. I don't know why I ran to the middle of a peanut field and fell to my knees and asked God's forgiveness.

    Invested prayer: You know who God is.
    Invested prayer: I have many people tell me what to do.
    Invested prayer: My talk with God involves waiting on his answer.
    Invested prayer: Showing others that God is a spirit.
    Invested prayer: God has been talking to you, learn to hear his voice.
    Invested prayer: Not telling God but asking.
    Invested prayer: Learn to understand his word.
    Invested prayer: Telling others how you talk to God
    Invested prayer: In the name of Jesus Christ.

Keep My Heart, Keep Me All the Way

Margaret's Reflection

Deacon Cypress is always ready to teach, counsel, and interpret. His message on invested prayer led me to recall the opportunities I have experienced in teaching and learning biblical principles. First of all, I always attended Sunday school and vacation Bible school as a child. As I grew into adulthood, I became an advocate for religious retreats and religious conferences. I attended many women conferences, and I actually loved attending weekend retreats. These events strengthen my spiritual life. Most of the time I didn't want to leave the events because the experiences made me feel safe and secured from the world. I sincerely enjoyed the fellowships and the worshipping experiences. Sometimes I imagined that the experiences made me believe I was in heaven.

I used the opportunities to develop confidence to share and even lead in various topics. I also gained enjoyment acting as a delegate, representing my church. My motive for these adventures was to grow spiritually. Remembering and associating childhood experiences can have a great impact on your physical growth. I have heard it said that there is a devil on every level. I remembered how to invest in prayer during life's struggles. This lesson came to me out of a Baptist convention. I was nineteen and remembered the sermon entitled "Making the Best of a Bad Situation." Emphasis from this sermon was to trust God with all of life's challenges, and our prayers must be sincere from our heart. I even had the opportunity to deliver a message entitled "Five Dangerous Prayers."

I have enjoyed and I'm extremely grateful for my salvation, but I'm still struggling achieving a stronger degree of sanctification.

I'm not where I should be, but I am not where I used to be.

Invested Prayers

A Message from Reverend Calvin Rideau Sr.

"Confess your faults one to another and pray one for another, that ye may be healed. The effectual fervent prayer of a righteous man availeth much" (James 5:16 KJV).

In this passage of scripture, James reminds the people that their lives are bound by more than mutual cares or affection but above all by their shared relationship with God. The community is therefore to respond to threats of sickness or sin by gathering in prayer. Why? Because the prayers of the masses are very powerful and productive. Thus, healing occurs and joy is experienced.

Margaret's Reflection on the Message

My most memorable experience of effectual praying is very different from my other experiences. I recalled meeting my Grandma Caldonia in downtown Baltimore on nine consecutive Mondays to attend a half-hour prayer service called Novena. This was at a Catholic church named St. Alphonsus. We would attend for the purpose of rendering our own personal petitions to God. My invested prayer included high school graduation, college, marriage, and becoming a mother. My heart rejoices until this very day; God answered those consistent prayers in that setting. This experience taught me consistency, commitment, discipline, and knowledge of a different type of worship. I appreciated the opportunity to compare my chosen form of worship to this experience and developed respect without my conversion of the Catholic denomination. I am receptive of most denominations that worship the Trinity, accepting Jesus as Lord and King, his death, burial, and resurrection. Jesus is all this world to me.

My Testimony

Rev. Kevin Blane

Born October 12, 1985, I was the third of four children born to Daniel and Laura Blane. I was blessed with two hardworking parents who taught us discipline and how to respect others. Early in life, my father's walk with the Lord got stronger, and he became a deacon, and soon after he accepted his calling to preach. I was around the age of eight or nine years old. So yes, the title of preacher's kid was added to my name. It's safe to say that life wasn't normal, but that's not a bad thing.

We had to go to church, we had to participate, and we loved it. It helped shape and mold us; it gave us that strong foundation. I played the drums, I danced, I directed the choir over my teenage and adolescent years, I was always by my father's side. I loved the church, I loved to worship, but most of all I loved the Lord. Now around the age of sixteen or seventeen, you try to find yourself as a young man, starting to date girls, hang out with friends, and experimenting with things. You feel grown enough to have an opinion and feel the urge to talk back to your parents or think you have it all figured out. I was not a bad child at all, but I didn't want to be the perfect church boy anymore.

I left for college, got away from the church, and all I cared about was girls, parties, drinking. The fast life felt so much more fun than doing what I was taught. However, that life comes with a price. My grades began to drop, I was not attending classes, and I was forced to drop out of college. I had to come home, face my parents, and deal

Invested Prayers

with the real world. My father, like many, gave me two options; get a job and help with bills or I can get out. I did find work, but I had no understanding of how the world works. I just wanted a roof over my head, food to eat, a cell phone, a car, and I would blow the rest of my paycheck on alcohol, clubs, and junk. My mom would often say, "Son, you are living for the weekend, and it will catch up with you, and life is going to pass you by."

You don't want to live by rules when you are in your twenties, so I moved out, got a place with some friends, but the cycle continued: get paid, spend it all, do it again next week. Finally, luck ran out; a lady friend said she was pregnant by me. Immediately, a light switch came on and I had to do better, I was going to be a father. I had a great father, and I wanted to follow his example. I did everything right by this lady. We had our place, I had a good job, I went to every appointment, and nine months later here comes a baby girl. There was one problem: the child was not mine. I was crushed and fell into depression, and life started to spiral downhill. Now through all of this, I still went to church regularly; I just had the understanding that no matter what, you can go to God, pray, fellowship, and things will work out. A young girl whom I've known all my life came into the picture, and she encouraged me during those dark times. We were best friends and we brought out the best in each other. She was preparing to go to college, and I decided that I would try the military. I joined the United States Army in 2010.

It was my first time away from family and friends, all on my own; the only person I knew to talk to was God. It was at this point that God would finally have me right where he wanted me. I began to pray daily, I started to talk to others about Christ, and I was even allowed to conduct my own Bible study on Sundays. A group of about ten male soldiers would surround my bunk, and we would have church. I was eager to get down and get back close to home, but God knew I still had a long way to go, so instead, I received orders to South Korea. I proposed to my best friend and told her we would get married once I returned.

Once again here I am in another country far away from everyone, on my own. At one point, I lost my way again, got caught up in the party scene, and I was out enjoying the big lights of South Korea.

I always loved to rap and do music, and I started to get back into it, but I was making songs for the world and the clubs and not for God's glory. I was back to the old me; the only difference was I was in the army and no longer depressed. The year went by, and the army sent me to Fort Sill, Oklahoma. This was my true turning point, for I was with my wife, and we were only five hours from our families. So we went home often, and we had that support system as a young couple. The first thing we did was find a church knowing that we needed God in our lives. We were blessed by God to walk into New Jerusalem Baptist Church in Lawton, Oklahoma.

Now we were young and far from perfect, but we knew we need to be around some saved people and in a church house. We went every Sunday. They loved us like family, helped us as a young couple, made sure we had everything we needed. It got to the point where I joined the choir, played the drums again, and even joined the men's ministry. Life was awesome, and God was blessing us tremendously. In 2013 my wife, Latrecie, and I, welcomed our first daughter, Lyrical Faith Blane. I was a father and taking care of my family. My pastor decided to elevate me to a deacon of the church. I served well, but something was pulling at me to do more. I accepted my calling to preach the gospel and on September 16th, 2015, I preached my initial sermon, "You're Check Engine Light Just Came On." I preached on how Jesus came to call the sick, not just those who were well. How we act like everything is okay on the outside, but we are a mess on the inside. Over the years, I have served as associate pastor in Hawaii, and most recently I have relocated to Fort Eustis, Virginia, and I now serve as youth pastor of First Baptist Church Morrison, in Newport News, Virginia. We have three beautiful daughters, I am going on eleven years of military service, and currently working on my master's degree. I still make music but it's gospel music, and I now give God all the praise. My next goal is to become an army chaplain so I can continue to minister to soldiers and their families. Life is not easy, I'm far from perfect, but the God I serve is a healer and a restorer. He was always with me even in my low points. That foundation I had as a child stuck with me and no matter what I knew how to call on his name, and now I stand here as Rev. Kevin J. Blane, and a Christian hip-hop artist.

I Never Could Have Made It Without God on My Side

Harvey's Response

I reflected on my journey after reading Minister Blane's testimony. My journey was filled with alcohol and drugs. My first thoughts were on my father, Eugene Mears, better known as Pick Mears, an alcoholic who managed a shot house in our house. We were constantly surrounded with neighborhood people and kin drinking, smoking, gambling, and all sorts of activities they called having fun. I didn't use these exposures as an excuse for my drinking habit. I did think it was normal. I found out that drinking alcohol eased my pains of being motherless, of being rejected so many times, and the pains of loneliness, especially when I was broke. Despite our weakness, binding, and complicated relationships with a woman named Cynthia, we lived together for years. I will never forget the time I had been clean for a year or two, and she told me that she liked me better when I was on drugs. She wasn't an addict but just a poor supporter of my recovery mission. I guess I could have been called a functional addict. I had to work to support myself so I could buy my drugs and pay my rent. I would get paid on Friday and wake up broke on Saturday. Through it all, I never forgot the prayers my grandmother invested for my protection, my releasing destructive thinking, recovering from my sinful attitude and to return to God. I can tell you those prayers were answered.

I have been in active recovery since November 22, 2008. Our testimonies connected with marriage. At fifty-three years old, God gave me a wife. I never thought this would happen to me. Most of the women I thought may be a possibility of marrying always interrupt the relationships with cheating incidents, lies, and three of them died. One woman had moved to Georgia and we were seriously talking about marriage, so she had me visit her church here in Newport News for the purpose of making our relationship stronger. When I made the visit, an old lady greeted me and at the end of the service, she handed me a book. I forgot the specific title, but I remembered the title included the word *warlock*, and she said, "We want you to become our leader." I called my friend in Georgia and asked many questions about this book and the worship experience. I received unclear answers. I placed the book on a shelf in my closet, never making any attempts to read any of it. A religious lady told me to get rid of the book because it sounded like witchcraft. Just think, I was seriously planning to move to Georgia to marry this woman who had abnormal views of religion and practices as I knew religious worship to be. I truly believe that God had his hands on me in rejecting this proposal. I thank God for the wife he gave me.

If I Can Help Somebody, My Living Will Not Be in Vain

Margaret's Response

Frustration, frustration, and more frustration are what I experienced in trying to get my children and my grandchildren go to church. When I was their ages, I really enjoyed church. I had fun at church. Each decade gave me different motives for attending church. During my teenage years, my primary interest was the choir marching and singing. Naturally, we experienced social activities, puppy love relationships, dating, and peer gossiping. We also took what we heard seriously. I remembered my Sunday school teacher said, "You shouldn't use profanity to words when angry." As a young adult, I became more serious about my worship and developed an appetite for singing on the choir and teaching Sunday school. I enjoyed this decade; however, I became curious about what I was missing, which was the clubs, dancing, parties, and drinking. Some of my church members mingled with me in these adventures. The saints called this indulgence, straddling the fence. During my middle-age decade, I developed a deeper and stronger relationship with Jesus. I forgot to mention I was baptized at the age of twelve and received Jesus in my life.

Now, as an aged woman, I am seeking holiness. Titus 2:3 gives me direction to behave in holiness and be a teacher of good things. I strive to be spirit-led, true in my worship, consistent in my walk, disciplined in my behavior. I want to increase my faith, overcome any fears, be content in all situations yet be eager to accept God's will and purpose for my life at my current age of seventy-four. I'm pressing on the upward way. New heights I'm gaining everyday while trusting God every step of the way.

Prayer

Jane O. Valentine

"Father, I stretch my hand to thee, no other help I know…"
"As I pray this morning, I am asking you to bless my children."

As I pen these words, my thoughts and mindset go back to my youth; the effects of my father's words in his prayer are still alive and being manifested to this day. When he prayed, he never asked for God to bless himself, but he repeated, "God bless my children." I do believe God saved all of my father's blessings in reserve and gave them one by one to each of his children when needed. As each child reached adulthood, they never wanted for anything true; there were struggles but not want. It has been passed onto the grandchildren through their parents.

My first prayer of remembrance happened in my early school years. I was a member of the glee club, and we were going to the college to sing on a program. I needed $1.25 to go on the bus. My mother said she did not have the money, so I could not go. I prayed all week that somehow God would send me the money for the trip. On Sunday, my father said someone asked him to drive them some place and pay him. He paid for the ride and had the money to give me for the trip.

Another answered prayer. Lord, let my mother live until I get grown. I do not want to be taken out of school to tend the younger children. I had classmates whose mothers had died, and they did have a hard time. One of them used to cry every day after her mother died. Also, I prayed that I live to see my children well grown and secured to take care of themselves.

Well, answered prayers for both situations.

This is my prayer, amen.

Sweet Hour of Prayer

Harvey's Response

Jane's testimony made me think of people I know whom I thought were prayer investors for me. Grandma was definitely my major prayer investor. I witnessed time after time the manifestations of her prayers, especially when I was arrested. Grandma bailed one of my cousins out of jail, and he decided he was going to run. Grandma had my brother and I hog-tie him and return him to the police station. This reaction from Grandma gave her the title of bounty hunter by a few policemen. She was short, stout, and very, very strict. Sometimes I even thought she was mean with love. I also remembered that she carried a .22 pistol in her pocket for her protection. My aunts and uncles were praying people, and I am sure I was included in their prayers. I know my wife has invested many prayers for me and our marriage because we have prayed together daily in our morning devotions.

Somebody Prayed for Me

Margaret's Response

I was blessed to know my maternal great-grandmother Hicks. Her Indian physical traits dominated her black American traits. Grandma Hicks loved reciting poems in public settings. She prayed continuously at church and at home. Looking back, I am amazed at her agility to kneel on eighty-year-old knees in prayer as often as she did. Most of my night prayers are said from my bed in fear that if I bowed down on my knees, I may not be able to get up without help. She lived to teach four generations of family members to pray with supplication and gratitude. My paternal grandmother had a strange name: Caldonia. We had a very strong spiritual bond. I lived in her home for years. Manipulating the move from my teenage opposition of my mother's fourth pregnancy, Grandma Caldonia had two sons whom I know she was in constant prayer for. She had left my grandfather due to verbal and physical threats. She had a live-in boyfriend named Joe. I never saw them share the same room, nor the same bed.

When I was eleven years old, he touched me inappropriately, forcing a kiss on my lips. No, I didn't tell anyone in fear it would hurt my grandmother too much and of the guilt of not telling because I liked the feelings of being loved by a man. I suppressed these feelings until I was a grown woman, and I heard Joyce Meyer's story of sexual abuse by her own biological father. For the first time, I confessed my reactions and feelings to God and asked for forgiveness. My grandmother allowed her tears to express her hurts and disappointments as she would sing "I Must Tell Jesus" and "Hold to God's Unchanging

Hand." She would also cry tears of happiness as she sung "He's Sweet I Know," "I Will Trust in the Lord," "What a Friend we Have in Jesus," and "Precious Lord." On any given day, you could find grandma singing and praying. These observations instilled resources of peace and hope within myself at various stages of my life.

My maternal grandmother, Pinkie Perry, was another prayer warrior. She was married twice. She had two children and both died in the year of 1968. Both children died suddenly. My mother died of a heart attack in January of 1968, and her brother died in July of the same year from drowning during a fishing trip. We called Grandma Pinkie "Nana." She lived in the Bronx, New York, with her husband, Joel Perry. He was like a real grandfather. I eagerly accepted the opportunity to live with them shortly after my high school graduation. Diligently seeking adequate employment and meeting rejections time after time, I gave up and returned to Baltimore. However, I took with me their daily routines of practicing daily Bible reading and praying.

I heard my mother; Annie Boone, pray short yet sincere prayers such as "Lord, Help Me," "Lord, Have Mercy," and "Lord, Give Me Strength." These prayers were rendered with her gasping, asthmatic breath. I know and believe she also prayed for her children and her husband, Sweeney Boone, whom she couldn't locate most of the time because he was working as a merchant seaman. Daddy appeared extremely quiet when sober but loud and responsive under the influence of alcohol. I am unsure of his prayer life.

There were many other kinfolks and friends whom I believe invested prayers for me, including Jane Valentine, my spiritual big sister.

My Testimony

Debra Seletta Biggs

I want to start off by thanking the Lord. He has been so good to me. He has blessed me with a new vehicle and also has allowed me to pay off my condominium.

I wrote down on a piece of paper in the year of 2020 the things I wanted to accomplish in 2021. God blessed me with my truck in 2020. I am so proud of myself, and this was a true blessing to me. I'm thankful for what he has done for me. I give him all of the praise for being a good God and a blessing in my life.

Thank you, Lord, for all you have done for me.

Praise Is What I Do

Margaret's Response

There was a period in my life that was full of worrying and complaining. This period was immediately erased by a mission trip I went on in October 2010 to Haiti. It was more than evident that the country had suffered a major earthquake because the remnants were quite visible. After witnessing families sleeping on dirt and even mud sometimes, it made me appreciate my bedroom and all of its old furniture. What a blessing to have a queen-size mattress to sleep on at home. What a blessing to be able to adjust my room temperature, as opposed to sleeping on rocks, stones, sticks, and bugs, and maybe under a tent, in all kinds of weather. I could turn on my kitchen or bathroom faucet to get clean running water, as opposed to carrying a bucket or a large barrel of water for miles on my head. I saw so many homes that were poorly built, unworthy of being called a shack.

After witnessing so much devastation, I was truly aware of my blessings that awaited me back home. It was uplifting to join with the worshipping services in a marginally structured church. Those residents worshipped God as if they were millionaires. They appeared to have put their whole hearts in praising Jesus. It was also inspiring to see so many missionaries from all over the United States lending a helping hand to this desperately needed country. It is much worse with direct confrontation. My praises are deeper and more sincere after this trip to Haiti. I am still investing prayers for the people in Haiti. I would have to mention there was wealth observed in Haiti. We were assigned to a rural, partially developed area. Cows, horses, and goats roamed the streets freely. Just a few people were dressed as professionals or government representatives displaying wealthy appearances. Once again, I must comment on their spiritual wealth; the Haitians we observed were spiritually wealthy in their praise and worship services. This mission trip has elevated me to a more sincere level of gratitude and a deeper appreciation of all that God has done for me. It has also made me more cognitive of things I may have taken for granted. I am glad we didn't go into the inner rural areas because I was told living conditions were much more devastating than the area we visited. May the Lord continue to bless them with aid from missionaries and various church-sponsoring groups.

You Can't Beat God Giving

Harvey's Response

I have so many stories I could reveal pertaining to things that were taken from me, things that I have loaned out and have never been returned to me, the time and money I used to help people who showed no gratitude in any form. I am grateful for all God has done for me. He has restored and replaced all that the enemy has taken. I am also grateful for any acts of love and kindness coming from friends or foes. It's important for me to adapt a lifestyle wherein people can see Christ in me. Most of the material things I have acquired came from my invested prayers to God, but I believe my character and behavior changes were the results primarily from my grandma's invested prayers. I know she prayed that I would hang around the right people. She prayed that I wouldn't get involved with drugs and commit fornication. Grandma prayed for my protection from the streets and the wickedness it shared. She also prayed that I would be a hard worker, find jobs that would make me financially independent, and of course she prayed I would find a good wife. These prayers were rendered for my siblings as well. I am sincerely grateful because God heard her invested prayers and answered them.

To God Be the Glory

Margaret's Response

Debra's testimony made me think of an experience I had in the importance of keeping a prayer journal. I was driving in my brand-new car that I prayed to purchase, but the prayer wasn't answered until a year later. I had forgotten that I prayed for the car that I really wanted and had accepted a car less desirable. *I praised God for both cars, realizing that God answers prayer in his time. A prayer journal would have served as a reminder of my faith and strengthened my beliefs. I can testify that since I have transformed and allowed God to have full reign over every aspect of my life, this is my best life ever!*

I also learned that the truths we have been taught must be put into practice and placed in obedience. Prayers must be believed when rendered. Patience must be utilized after the prayers have been invested. There are times when prayers are answered and the prayer investor doesn't live to see the manifestations of the answered prayers, as described in the eleventh chapter of Hebrews.

He's a Healer

Arnika Nichols's Testimony (Romans 8:28)

And we know that all things work together for good to them who love God, to them who are the called according to his purpose.

When the voice of God has told you *no* about something, you move in its direction anyway.

I moved to Maryland in 2012 to attend an HBCU. The plan was to get the degree and return home; however, I met him in junior year. I was coming home from a night out with girlfriends. I parked my car and began to walk toward my apartment unit. A truck was pulling in as I was walking. The lights glared in my direction, I turned, witnessed this truck almost pull up on the curb as the driver was attempting to pull into a parking space. He was distracted staring at me. I continued to walk and picked up speed. The driver got out and addressed me in an effort to get my attention. This was the beginning of one of many life lessons and a turning point in my maturity and development as a woman.

I was smitten with him, he held my attention, he wasn't aggressive, he said he knew the Lord, he was a PK (preacher's kid), so I thought this must be a situation for me to explore. We liked one another, we enjoyed one another's company, he had a job, transportation, and his own place. Independence made him appealing—after all, that's what makes a man, right? Lol, I had so much to learn. Never mind that he already had two children by separate women and, while dating, I learned of a third child who was born when we first met. It's funny how we feel it in our gut when something is not right. That still, small voice… We know when there are secrets, information comes our way that we aren't seeking—when you are not invited on the family trips or to the class reunions, when you meet the friends and they seem to have inside jokes, when you begin to have issues with other women who hate you because you are in the position she thinks she wants to be in only to realize that she was once you in his life, when you have to request to meet his family after a significant amount of time has passed and when you're in a relationship in your mind but the flow of the relationship just isn't flowing as it should.

I had a habit of aiding my process, making it fit into this mold or something that I thought would be suitable to those whom I was accountable to. After all, I knew that I had a calling in my life since I was a child. I was told many times in various situations that I couldn't do what everyone else did because I was set apart. When my choices in life went against what I felt God's will for my life was, the consequences were life-altering. This relationship had an impact on a decade of my life. There were many ups but hard downs; I loved him. We became pregnant twice; the first time I decided to abort and that was one of the toughest moments in my life among others. I flew across the country, and with support of some friends, I experienced it alone. I returned because I was in college. There were periods of being on and off through the duration of the experience. He cheated, I cheated; we continued in a cycle that stole time from the both of us. Finally, there was a situation when I discovered he was on a date with someone other than me, so I stopped taking his calls and began to date someone else.

I told myself this time would be different; I thought I would make better choices this time. I was tired of the cycle that I just walked away from. My behavior did not change, my selfish intentions and flesh guided me right into the reality of having to tell both of these men that I was pregnant. The following months were full of me working to get my life together, repentance, transparency, and self-reflection. God's grace and mercy surrounded me. God made sure I was connected to people who extended nothing but love, compassion, and support during the duration of my pregnancy. My mother flew in when it was time for me to give birth. She stayed one week and a portion of the time we were trying to figure out how to make me go into labor. I gave life to a healthy baby girl. My mother was gone two days later, and I remember asking God what I was supposed to do now. I was terrified yet in love with my daughter at the same time. I had to deal with the humiliation of paternity testing and the reality that the person who really wanted to be her father and supported me during the duration of my pregnancy was not her father.

My child changed my life in a major way. God knew that she would become my "ram in the bush." I wanted her to have a family and not be raised in a broken family. Her father and I tried to live together, play house, and operate in the mode of being a "happy family." The enemy will mask a person or situation to almost fit what we think is right for us, and because it's close enough to the true reality of what we want, we settle for the mock version of the real thing. The truth of the matter is we were miserable. Yes, there was love; yes, we experienced some good times, but at that time we were two immature, irresponsible, rebellious, and reckless individuals who were not looking to obey God's will for our lives. We did what we wanted to do at the expense of one another. I lost sight of my purpose, I managed money poorly, I had major trust issues, I was broken, I didn't value my worth or my body for that matter. I was superficial and in denial.

God loved me enough to allow me to become so uncomfortable that I was forced out. At one point, I was juggling being a mom, an injured partner, broke but working in an environment that was indescribably stressful. I knew my child's father was seeing someone, but I had no proof; I literally felt like I was suffocating. I was unhealthy mentally and physically, and I was pulled in many directions. I knew I was breaking when I headed out one morning to take my baby to school and a little boy ran out in the street and I hit him with my car. I got out to console him and a crowd of people began to swarm me. The child's brother approached me upset and threatened to harm me. There were some men who spoke with him and encouraged him to allow his mother and I to talk. I recall his mother telling me to stop crying because "he never listens," she said. "He was supposed to be on the sidewalk walking with his sister," she went on the say. "He ran from her." I remember thinking she was crazy. I was livid with her for saying this to me. I just wanted him to be okay. The little boy got up and was able to walk. Officers were on the scene and the school was less than a block away, so I recall many people moving in the direction of the school while trying to see what was happening. I gave the child's mother my information and told her to call me. I remember just wanting to fix it. I felt sick to my stomach; it was surreal to me. At that time, I didn't have insurance, and my license was expired. The officer whom I spoke with was more than kind and extremely supportive. I remember having the car pulled along the sidewalk, and I left it right where it was. When I think about how good God has been to me, how he covered me in my mess, tears of adoration streamed from my face as I recalled this moment in my life. The reality is that situation could have been so much worse than it was.

I walked my daughter to school, and the administrators consoled me, reassuring me that everything was going to be okay. My close friend and daughter's father left work. We all met at the house. The officer came by my home to check on me and reported that the little boy had minor scrapes. The reports from the neighbors were that he ran out in front of my car—thank God I was not speeding—so when the car bumped him and he fell into the street, the impact was not devastating to his body. Nothing was broken, and his mother called with the same information. This was my breaking point! When returning to work, I stepped into the office of a colleague who has become family to me. You know how God assigns people to your life and perfectly places people in a time and space of a journey that thrusts you into another level that you otherwise would not have moved into. Well, this was the beginning of that moment for me. I remember being in her office, and she just began to pray for me in a way that felt so personal; I felt like she was praying for herself or one of her own children. There was a sense of peace that came over me and gave me hope. She and I would connect daily; we prayed and encouraged one another. She always told me to listen for the voice of God and run for my life when God said, "Go!"

One evening, I was working late and I had to take some files from one side of the building to the other. I recall passing one of our security guards and heading into the computer room. I overheard the guard attempting to get my attention. I was heading back, and he stopped me. He asked me my name and began to speak to me as if he knew me. He shared the word that the Lord gave him about me and told me that I was "displaced." I was not supposed to still be in the demographic that I was in. It was complete confirmation for me because everything tied to me was failing at this point. I was barely existing. I even remember a friend of mine who warned me about moving in with my child's father before I did it. She told me she had a vision of me behind bars and my face looked unhappy.

I moved in anyway and years later my life, emotions, peace, and joy were all locked up, and I didn't know who I was anymore. I remember asking God to change my life. I thought I wanted to marry him, but I had no idea what I was asking for. He was not ready and did not want to marry me. Everything I put my hands to failed. My relationships and the life that I built was very hard to let go of, but I knew it was time to transition, and I knew that I had to move swiftly because my window of time was winding up. The guard who spoke the word of the Lord became a spiritual father figure to me, and my praying colleague became a spiritual mother. I told her about my encounter with him, and she avoided meeting him initially (something we laugh about often). We began to connect daily—meeting in the aisles at the job, in our cubicles, in the parking lot, capturing moments to encourage, share, worship, and speak on the goodness of God. I began to develop a thirst for the word, my strength was coming on. Before I knew, it my desires and patterns began to change.

I was contacted by someone whom I had not been in touch with for a while. She asked me if my child's father and I were separated because she saw him at a local casino with someone else. I came across a receipt at home one day while cleaning and noticed scratches on the hood of my child's father's truck—several signs and confirmation that he was now bold enough to see someone while I was living with him, helping with his children, and raising our daughter. I remember feeling like it was yet again confirmation. I was hurt but reassured that I needed to get out of the stagnant space I was in and better my life. It was time to heal. I called my mother and told her I was ready to move back home. I needed to book a flight and notify my employer that I was leaving. I submitted my notice of resignation; I told my spiritual mom and dad that I decided to be obedient and follow God's plan for my life. It was time to get into position.

I made so many choices based off of what I wanted that I changed the course of my life. Every message that I heard confirmed what was in my heart, every song I heard encouraged me and reminded me that I was special to God. I had a heart-to-heart with my child's father. There was a heaviness; a few months prior to my decision, he told me that he felt like I was going to leave. I remember saying that I would never leave and break the family up, yet there we were. It was if God prepared him as well. I'll never forget the day I told my spiritual mom and dad that I resigned and was leaving. Although the Lord used them to push me, it was if there was a shock factor. However, the joy of the Lord is our strength, and the three of us celebrated and rejoiced. I said goodbye to friends and family. It was not easy walking away from the very thing I thought I wanted to show God that my trust in him was greater. Before leaving, my spiritual mom and I ended up with matching dents on the back corner of our cars. The enemy was mad; we had a farewell lunch and laughed about it. I was blessed with spiritual books and some farewell gifts of reassurance.

A dear loved one purchased my ticket; the night before leaving, I felt empowered. I flew home with my baby and a few clothes to start my life over. When I returned to the West Coast, I remember there was an earthquake our first week back. It served as a sign that things were being shook up in the spirit. Within three months, God opened a door, and I began working in the field of education. I lived with my parents for six years. I healed, dealt with some internal struggles, became stronger. I watched God heal areas of my immediate bloodline. My mother and I are closer than ever and are able to be 100 percent transparent with one another; please know there is healing in that alone. My brother and I have had difficult conversations and dealt with our differences. I am watching him blossom into the man whom God called him to be, and I could not be more proud of his growth. I paid off a vehicle. My daughter and her father have a very special bond, and God blessed him and I to heal and be the closest of friends. We respect one another and focus on our daughters' well-being. Although there is distance, we are united, and God's grace has kept us.

Our daughter is bright, beautiful, strong, talented, gifted, and amazing. She has tapped into her spiritual gifts. She is firm and speaks with conviction regarding what she believes. I am proud that she can look at me and see the strength of the Lord. I have had an opportunity to speak to women about my journey. God has blessed me to work within my community and make a difference. Understanding that God has not even begun to show me all that he has in store, I am often reminded of how the Lord honors obedience. He has definitely had his hand on my life. As I reflect, I can't forget to mention I was molested most of my teen years. I recently discovered that my father struggles with addiction, and our relationship has been challenging—but God, he has given me compassion for others, and I am mindful of my behaviors and feelings toward others. God blessed my daughter and I with a cute little house that we love to hide away in. The space is full of peace, love, and joy.

There is an internal work happening down on the inside of me that is undeniable. Even in my hard spaces, God has found ways to reach me. He reassures me that he will never leave nor forsake me. I have questioned him, his existence, I have fallen short and thrown in the towel at times. I am not perfect, and I know that I am nothing without God. I have learned to be my authentic self because he knows me by my name. He knows exactly who I am and who he created me to be. I can now speak my truth and be bold and hold myself and others accountable. I can hold my head up and say I am a woman of integrity. I crave productive energy and refuse to stay stagnant. I have learned God's voice; there are many forms of how he speaks to me. I have also learned that he keeps close watch over what is dear to him.

No matter how we may stray, God is strategic in how he draws us near again. Although many people are around me, this walk can be lonely but fulfilling. I have my peace. I give him all of the glory for who I am, who I am becoming, and all that he is doing in me and through me. I am learning to be present. I am reminded that I am his hands and feet on the earth, and I will leave an imprint. I will close with this: when the Lord wakes me up each day, I imagine the enemy stomping and pouting, saying, "Not *her*!" Be reminded that the enemy seeks to devour. He's a thief, a murderer, and he is destructive, but he can't steal what God put your name on. He can't destroy what God made indestructible, and he can't kill what God has given life to. Shake it off and move forward in Christ! If I can do it, so can you. Be blessed! Live in the fullness of God! The Lord gave us permission to live in abundance, so go forth and live!

Every Time I Feel the Spirit

Harvey's response

My thoughts centered around an occasion. I had a real serious argument with a guy named Parker. We came very close to having a physical fight. Both of us were in the same rehabilitation program, and the entire residents of the program had to go to a parade downtown. I can't remember what the argument was about or how it got started. I do remember Parker sitting on the curb cursing me. After exchanging a few words of threats to each other, I decided to walk away to cool off. I also remembered thanking the Lord for giving me strength to walk away. The next day, after a group session, I approached Parker and offered an apology for my reactions. He did the same; we shook hands and hugged. Three days later, we received an announcement from the director telling us that Parker died riding his bike to drug court. All of us were shocked. I was so glad I had put my reputation aside and walked away from the confrontation. I was even happier that I apologized. God submitted his Holy Spirit and had me do the right thing.

Another occasion: a coresident tried to persuade me to go with him to his girlfriend's house. He wanted to introduce me to a friend of his girlfriend. I kept telling him no. The very next day we received the news; he had been shot at his girlfriend's house. I was sorry to hear the news, but I was glad my weakness for women didn't entice me to go with him. Grandma's invested prayers for my protection were still effective.

I also thought of my Uncle June being placed in my life as a guiding angel. When my daddy was too busy serving liquor and entertaining in his shot house from 6 a.m. until the last person left, late in the night, my uncle was usually around to help us and teach us carpentry skills. He and his wife, Lois, always remembered us on our birthdays and Christmas. I miss him, and I still want to be like him.

Precious Lord

Margaret's Response

God places people in our lives to achieve his will and his purpose. I had a tendency to give people who crossed my path a relationship title. When my sibling died, I sought out people for replacement and entitled them. There was one entitlement I declared in alignment with Titus 2:3, which states the characteristics of an aged woman. I found those characteristics in three Christian women in my life. I called them my spiritual mothers. Mother Baker allowed God to use her when my mother passed away. I was a young adult, and I am so grateful for the guidance and nurturing she extended to me. Mother Daisy Perry used her Bible knowledge, counseling experiences, nurturing, and training skills in assisting me through my first marriage. Mother Kirby is my current spiritual mother whom I may call anytime with any problem that needs Christian interpretation and guidance. These women were given wisdom and used it according to the Word.

I had many ladies I called my spiritual sisters—too many to list by names. We went to retreats together, we had Bible study together, we read and discussed religious books, and went to plays. We even traveled to various states. We laughed and cried together numerous times. We were always there for each other. I considered us as women in training to become spiritual mothers to a generation of young people desperately in need of spiritual guidance. Oh, how I love Jesus because he first loved me.

All of my pastors, past and present, have served as my spiritual brothers and leaders. I have learned to listen to their teachings and apply the messages to my life. I had to study the Word, meditate, and practice the teachings. Now, as an aged woman, I can confess; I am seeking holiness and disregarding carnality. Lord, I am truly striving to be the woman you would have me to be. I am striving to be spirit-led, true in my worship, consistent in my walk, disciplined in my behavior. I want to increase my faith, overcome my fears, and be content in all situations, yet be eager to accept God's will and purpose for my life.

I Need You

Margaret's Response

I am so happy that God put people in our lives to help us, advise us, and encourage us. I am very thankful for all of my spiritual mothers. They have had such an impact on my life, allowing God to use them according to his will and his purpose.

Unequally Yoked

Barbara Gurley

My testimony is living in a miserable young marriage with abuse, verbal and physical—a living nightmare that I thought would never end or would end in a disaster. I've always been in church as a child all the way to my adult life. I never wanted anything different—just be in the presence of the Lord. My getting married at the age of twenty-three years old, not knowing that people disguise themselves to get what they want, but also not knowing how to keep what I have or had—misery loves company.

Being the only child until the age of seventeen, I was a joyous and happy child growing into womanhood. I met my first husband at our place of employment, and he pursued me like no other admirer had ever done. He drew my attention, and we dated for about two years before marriage. He was more than nice; he was different from anyone I had dated before. He was older and way more excited in life, which excited me. We got married, and on the wedding night, he addressed me in a way he had never done before: in an abusive way. I could not believe it, but I thought maybe it was the pressure from the wedding and everything that led up to the wedding.

Being married, I was abused in every way, mentally and physically. Going to church that said divorce was not an option, that it was too fast, that it was better to pray more, with families that took sides (my family could not stand him, and his family blamed me), no one could help me. That's when I was learning to put my trust in God; I knew he would work things out. But I did not turn all of it over to

God. I passed the test for the military and was trying to run from this marriage as fast as I could. Finding out I had to sign our children over to his custody made me change my mind about the military. I prayed a lot, read my bible but not with a clear understanding. I asked a lot of questions about marriage, not being able to figure out why he was so unhappy; he had two beautiful children, a nice place to live, a car, jobs, a wife who loved him, but that was still not enough. I continued going to church believing that someday God would deliver me from this nightmare (marriage). He could not understand why I smiled all the time, even in my pain of the abuse. I would cry to the lord and tell him about all my troubles; I did not believe I deserved any of it.

People came into my life and gave me good counsel to help me along my journey. One said, "pick up your cross and carry it." That made me realize, as we talked, that I would have trials and tests that I would have to go through—just take everything to God. Another told me, "This too shall pass." Someone else told me, "The end if better than the beginning." Having this wisdom and a relationship with Jesus, the Son of the living God, gave me strength to ensure, and boldness set in.

I began to give him scripture about my marriage, love, and shared my feelings to him. But he did not change, and I prayed for a way of escape. We lost our apartment, and I had to go stay with a family member. He in turn stayed with his mother and father, and after a short while moved in with a woman. After he gave me an ultimatum to come back to him without any signs of change, I said no. He went on to stay with the woman. I stepped out in faith with Jesus leading and guiding me, along with the freedom of life—no more bondage, no more fear for my life, and it felt good. With time came the healing and manifesting of my mind, body, and soul. Years later, God gave me a gift: a wonderful loving husband who loves me and knows how to treat me, and I praise God for my gift.

My Hope Is Built on Nothing Less Than Jesus

Harvey's Response

I have not been legally married until I married Margaret, but I have had several common-law marriages. Through all of the live-in experiences, I can honestly declare I have not physically abused any woman. I had a bad temper, but I would react with verbal abuse. The heart I had during those days would lead me to be rude, disrespectful, and dirty with my responses. I refused to hit a woman because I saw my father physically abused my mother when I was a child; I was too young to stop him.

There was one occasion when I was living with a woman in Hopewell, Virginia; she disappeared for five days, no phone calls or text messages. When she left, the doctor had placed me on complete bed rest due to my neck injury. She knew I was sick but didn't care. This incident hurt because I fixed her house, which included repairing anything that was broken, painting all of her room, and reconstructing her deck. These projects were completed with my money. I even painted the exterior part of her house. When she came home with no excuse for her absence, I was furious. I grabbed her and sat her on top of the dresser. I wanted to hit her or slap her, but I just left and returned to Newport News.

A week later, I was hospitalized for an abscess, and this woman had sex with my twin brother. That was definitely the end of our relationship. I have had several fights with men who even look as if they were going to hit a woman. Some of these men were total strangers.

I will never forget the incident I stopped a man from really beating a woman. As I was on the ground fighting him, the woman hit me with her shoe.

Yield Not to Temptation

Margaret's Response

I really related to Barbara Gurley's testimony based on an unequal marriage. My first marriage lasted in time and in time only: for thirty years and five months. I wish I could say I prayed my way out of that marriage, but I cannot say that. I prayed with a weak belief and a stronger desire to fix myself. I chose to fight for the marriage through game-playing and pretending we had a close-to-perfect marriage. Robert was a hard worker, a good provider, and he went along with me wholeheartedly to adopt our daughter, Erica. Remember my dream? I wanted to be a mother. This marriage made me lose my identity, lowered my self-esteem, and compromised my biblical principles. I disregarded my sins and played "what's good for the goose is good for the gender." Momma always told me two wrongs don't make it right. I never knew of Momma cheating on my father. She spent her time raising four children and surviving a chronic asthma condition, but we had evidence that my father was a cheater. Despite my father's infidelity, I loved my daddy until he died in 1987. My reflection allowed me to forgive and release perpetual love for him to this very moment.

I irresponsibly rationalized my marriage according to my will, my thinking, my insecurities against limited biblical principles. My family and I had developed a once-a-week religion. We went to church on Sundays but failed to read or discuss the Bible during the week. Most of the time we forgot Sunday's sermon by the time we reached home on the same day. Looking back, I could always acclaim having an active prayer life. There were always situations warranting prayer. My husband didn't make me feel good enough to make him feel content to be loyal and faithful to one woman. My defense was the painful memories of my mother's marriage to my father, who collected women from every port he visited. My father was a merchant seaman who left at least two babies in foreign countries. One baby was born in Barcelona, Spain, and the other in Kingston, Jamaica. I used these memories to take revengeful reactions against my husband, Robert. I promised myself that I would never allow a man to cheat on me, having concrete proof of the cheating.

One occasion lies paramount in my attitude; I was admitted to the hospital and was diagnosed with a disruptive spleen. I was partying with my so-called friends and came home at four in the morning. Robert was more than furious. As I was stretched out on the sofa, Robert drew his fist back, motioning to hit me. I rolled over to duck the blow and I hit the marble coffee table next to me. Glory be to God; I was treated for four days in the hospital without any surgery. We separated after my discharge, and I returned to Baltimore with Erica. Robert promised to take legal action if I didn't return to New York with our baby. The following years were full of ups and downs, but at least I learned to avoid creating problems because I was a mother. My mother endured the pains for the sake of her children. She stayed married so we could be a family intact.

I can testify just as Barbara has that the Lord answered prayers and provided me with an unbelievable man as my second husband.

My Testimony

Audrey Morton

My name is Audrey M., and I have a testimony. I am a seventy-eight-year-old widow and mother. I have come through many hard trials and tribulations, but I'm still standing tall. I married at the early age of sixteen to a non-Christian gentleman. I thought that my love was strong enough to turn him around. Well, it didn't work. During the period of raising my kids, I was sickly and in and out of the hospital often. I thank God for having a praying and supportive mother who was always standing in the gap for me. As my family became adults (two girls and two boys), I experienced their incarcerations many times. That was such a hardship for me because my husband was not around much of the time. He claimed his home was with us, but he did not stay around us often.

Moving forward as time passed, I was able, through God's help, to pick up the pieces of my life, go to work, and make a better life for myself. I bought a home—hallelujah! Later I was stricken with breast cancer, went through chemo for a five-year period, and recovered. Praise the Lord!

I was given the gift of music, and it has carried me through these trying times. My ministering in song has been a blessing to so many others, and it has helped me as well. Now my children have turned their lives around, and they are now walking with the Lord. I've lost my mother, my husband, and my two sons. Their deaths were devastating to me. It's been hard trying to go on, but by the grave of God, he has brought me through.

Last year's diagnosis was multiple melanoma, which is a cancer of the bone marrow. To this date, there is no cure for this disease, only remission. My doctor said he should have me in remission within a year, and my life span should be about five years. I started chemo last August and in March I was in remission. That took me only seven Months. My doctor was in shock because that was not the norm. I said to the doctor, "You don't know my God."

In November, my cancer returned. I am waiting for the next form of treatment. I will find out next Wednesday. I'm praying to God for healing, and I know he is true to his word. Therefore, I have no doubt that he will work it out in my favor.

In conclusion, I am living to live again. I am enjoying my life and living it to the fullest. I love God, and I have surrendered my life to him because he has never failed me yet. I say trust God with all your heart, and he will give you the desires of your heart.

God bless!

What a Friend We Have in Jesus

Harvey's Response

I wish I had the gift to sing, but I don't have that gift. But I can make a joyful noise unto the Lord who has had his hands on me throughout my life. I do have gratitude. Once again, the minister who stood in the catwalk of the jail cells, receiving all sorts of disgusting abuse, yet he ignored the abuse. He completed his mission strong and determined. To this very day, I admire his strength. I want to be strong in the Lord. I want to increase the love I have for myself, conquering all negative behavior. I want to have strong determination to move forward despite any obstacles. It is important for me to have the right motives for my actions and reactions. I want to live so God can use me.

I know my past has been less desirable and very punitive. I realize my past is just what it says, the past. God has forgiven me, and I have forgiven myself. Now I can declare I am a recovering addict. I am ready to help any addict seeking help to reach the level of recovery. I realize recovery starts with a made-up mind to make a change. I had to invest prayers for consistency in recognizing I needed Jesus to make it. I had to identify triggers and avoid them. My triggers were beer, women, and drugs. A family reunion took place, and all my cousins were drinking. I decided I was a grown man, and I could drink beer without claiming active addict status. I was in my eighth year of being clean, free from drugs and alcohol. That one beer was my trigger for reentry to the drug world. Sister Audrey, I can sing, I'm free. Praise the Lord, I'm free. No more chains holding me. God has given me a second chance.

One Day at a Time

Margaret's Response

Audrey has served my family as a soloist for many occasions. She sang "There's a Place for Us" at my wedding. I will always remember the solo she sang at my mother's funeral: "God Will Take Care of You." The lyrics to this hymn were received and believed by me. Those lyrics have delivered peace and strength to me in strenuous times. The most lonesome period of my life appeared at the beginning of my retirement. I retired on an incentive offer, a year before regular retirement. I moved to Newport News, Virginia. Robert and I had purchased a retirement home, in addition to our primary home, in Virginia. Both homes were manifestations of invested prayers. When I retired, I had been a widow for four years, and I moved to Virginia to be with Erica and her family. She refused to raise her children in New York after Robert's death.

Upon moving, I had almost depleted my savings. My first retirement check was far below what I expected. I was told there was a glitch in my agreement. Ten months later, I received a retroactive check. My retirement home was one step away from foreclosure. Once again, I received manifestations of invested prayers during the ten months I had to wait for that retroactive check.

I experienced another problem during the initial months of my retirement and move from New York to Virginia; my expectations of visitations from my daughter and grandchildren were not met. They lived in the primary house, and I lived in the retirement home. I did not acknowledge my daughter was grown with her own family, and she was not able to meet my time expectations. The enemy tried to tap negative feelings into our relationship, but thank God, invested prayers were answered. Erica has allowed me to be a real proud mother from her accomplishments and God's blessings.

Another important reflection took place in my seventh year of widowhood. I had decided, despite the fun and freedom I had experienced, that I missed and preferred marriage over singleness. My first boyfriend, Hurley Young, from my teen years, reappeared. Almost immediately, I decided Hurley would be my second husband. He and I discussed and explored the possibilities. Why not? He was divorced, and I was a widow. Both of us were retired teachers. Both of us were seeking a mate, a mate who loves the Lord. I was convinced Hurley was the mate for me. I invested prayers and asked the Holy Spirit for guidance. Hurley became ill, seriously ill with cancer. I spent many days with him during his suffering. I was with him when he passed. I had to accept the answer to this invested prayer and reinvest prayers for a husband. I will trust the Lord for all of my invested prayers. Hallelujah!

Miracles Witnessed

Marion Kirby

On January 5, 1967, while living in Washington, DC, late one evening, I received an unexpected phone call from my husband's job stating that he had expired, and I needed to come over to Maryland to identify his body. At that time, I did not drive, and my husband, Frank, had driven our car to work. My first cousin Dot and her husband, Ray, were living with us during this time. Ray got a neighbor to drive us over to Maryland. My husband had died of a massive heart attack.

When I got back home, I called Franklin Funeral Home and made arrangements to have his body picked up and brought back to Newport News, Virginia. The very next day, I made my way back to Giant Food Warehouse to talk to my husband's boss about his insurance policy. Frank's boss exalted words to me that my husband was lacking two days before his insurance came into maturity. This man was refusing to pay the insurance claim for my deceased husband.

I looked him straight in the eyes and said, "If I was white, you would have given me that money." I then turned around and made my way back home. With tears still flowing down my face, I called Mr. Franklin at the funeral home and told him that I did not know how I would be able to pay for his services. Praise God, hallelujah, Mr. Franklin's words to me were "not to worry." Although he would be unable to transport the body across state lines, he would line up another funeral home director to meet him at the state line to transfer the hearse carrying my husband from one vehicle in Maryland to his in Virginia. From that point, God and Mr. Franklin completely took over.

Mr. Franklin told me to let him know once I received my first social security check. My children and I had moved back to Newport News. I called him when my first check came in. He looked at the check I had and told me to just give him $200 and keep the rest to take care of my children.

My son Tyrone, who was born October 29, 1960, should have started grade school in 1966, but because his birth month was October, he was not allowed to start until the following school year, in the fall of 1967. At that time, children had to have a physical exam by a doctor before they could start school. During Tyrone's exam, the doctor discovered a hole in his heart that he was most likely born with. It was about the size of a fifty-cent coin. Tyrone needed to go to a heart specialist.

I made an appointment with the top heart surgeons in Newport News, Virginia, Dr. Pope Grier. After Tyrone was examined by Dr. Grier, I was told that he was still very young and could wait a few years before having to have the surgery. With my husband having recently died of a massive heart attack, I felt uneasy with waiting a few years for Tyrone's surgery, so I called our primary physician, Dr. Henry Ware.

Dr. Ware examined Tyrone and promptly made an appointment for evaluation at the Medical College in Richmond, Virginia. I got a friend, Harold Langford, to take us to the appointment since I still did not drive. On the way to Richmond, his car broke down, and we missed the appointment. Once home, I called Dr. Ware right away and told him what happened. He told me not to worry, then made another appointment for Tyrone.

This time, I depended on my heavenly Father to get us there because he had never failed me yet. After a thorough examination by the doctor at the Medical College, the doctor explained to me that Tyrone was born with a hole in his heart. Generally, if this happens, as the child grows, the hole closes, but Tyrone's had not. Tyrone would need surgery as soon as possible to repair this hole, and he would probably need to stay in the hospital for two weeks. I agreed.

This would be the longest two weeks of my life. I was told that Tyrone would go into surgery at six in the morning. The day of the surgery I woke up early and got my bath. When I returned to Tyrone's room, he was gone. The surgical team had arrived earlier than I was told and taken my son off to surgery. I could not eat. All I could do was pray, trust, and believe. I waited for Tyrone in the waiting room on the same hospital floor that he was having surgery on. I noticed a jigsaw puzzle on the waiting room table that was a thousand pieces. The outer edges of the puzzle were already in place. I started working on that puzzle in an attempt to keep focused. The only times I got up from that puzzle were to use the restroom and to check at the nurse's station about my son.

The nurse told me that she would let me know when Tyrone was out of surgery. It wasn't until around seven that evening that they brought my son out of surgery. I had finished the puzzle. I stood at the elevator door waiting for the doors to open. When they did, I saw Tyrone hooked up to a machine that looked like it had a hundred wires on it. Tyrone was taken to the ICU for a few days.

Now that I had seen my son and knew that he had made it out of surgery, I realized that I was hungry, so I went to the cafeteria. While waiting for the elevator, the Lord spoke to me. He said, "Why are you crying? Dry your eyes, the boy will be all right." From that time on, I knew it was my heavenly Father. My relationship with God had started when I was a young child. I knew his voice. I started to rejoice because I had just heard from my loving heavenly Father.

Now, when I think back over my situation, I recognize that my trip to the medical college in Richmond was an eye-opener for me. The enemy had crept in and stolen my joy by attacking my belief, my trust, and my faith. But even while doubts were working against me, something inside of me reminded me that true faith was the substance of things hoped for and the evidence of things I could not see.

When Tyrone and I had first gotten to that hospital, a nurse had asked us to come down the hall to the room where she was caring for a boy about Tyrone's age. Once we were settled into Tyrone's room, we made our way down to where the nurse was waiting for us. As soon as I opened the door and laid eyes on the child, I just stood in

Invested Prayers

the doorway and began to pray for this young boy. My son's condition, in comparison to this child's condition, was no more serious than a hangnail. This boy had had brain surgery, heart surgery, and a tube down his throat, I believe, for feedings.

Down the hall, another child who had drank some lye was there to have his esophagus replaced. In yet another room lay a pretty little girl on her bed with what resembled a large plastic balloon surrounding her and the bed. She had to stay in that bubble day in and day out. Last but not least, my son's roommate had also had open-heart surgery. They could not close his heart up.

God had let me know that no matter how bad our trouble may seem, there is always someone whose trouble is worse. After my stay in Richmond at the Medical College, I learned that God will never put more on you than you can bear, for what was supposed to be a two-week stay ended up only being a nine-day stay. Praise God!

We returned to Newport News, and I never had a problem with Tyrone. He gave me a scare once when he had a really bad nosebleed, but that is all. Here is the real miracle: when he went back to the doctor for his checkup, they took a chest x-ray. The doctor put the film up to the light so I could see it, and he said to me that there is no reason why Tyrone should not live to be fifty. I gave God all the glory and all the honor for the great thing he had done.

Come Ye Disconsolate

Harvey's Response

My reflections on Mother Kirby's testimony revisit September 25, 1969, the day my mother, Ola A. Mears, lied on our sofa, complaining of a headache, fell asleep, and never woke up. Harley, my twin, and I had great anticipation of celebrating our ninth birthday that very same day. When we couldn't wake our mother up, we went to Grandmom's. She came over and sent us to school. We were called out of school and returned home, but we went to our aunt's house instead of our own without knowing what was going on. Why was everyone crying?

Sudden death seems so unfair! Reviewing my family's history with death, there were so many sudden deaths. My grandmother dropped dead on the kitchen floor. I had stayed with my father, Eugene Mears, a whole week before he passed. I left him to do a favor for a friend, and before I could return, a cousin told me my father died. My sister Miccie was on life support until the plug was pulled, so she didn't make the list of sudden deaths. My Aunt Helen died from a heart attack behind the steering wheel of her car. My Uncle June left his home by ambulance and was pronounced dead shortly after reaching the hospital. My granduncle, Uncle Hercules, was at the doctor's office and passed there. My niece Anya was killed by her boyfriend, who turned around and killed himself in his car as he was running from the police.

✜ ✜ ✜ ✜ ✜ ✜ ✜ ✜ ✜ ✜ ✜ ✜ ✜ ✜ ✜

I'm Pressing On

Margaret's Response

My most reflective association with Minister Kirby's testimony was my season of widowhood. I will never forget the day my husband, Robert, passed away. Three different times, he had to be resuscitated. The third time, Robert was in dialysis, under a do-not-resuscitate decree, yet he was revived. When the nurse revealed this incident that described a miracle, two weeks later, the doctor called me at 6:55 a.m. to tell me Robert had expired ten minutes prior. On April 26, 2004, I became a widow. Although we had confessed, discussed, and reached some resolutions pertaining to our marital issues, guilty memories lingered. We had actually forgiven each other and prayed to God for forgiveness, individually and as a pleading couple. I was so grateful we had the opportunities to accomplish that mission.

No one told me that memories of their deceased spouse could and would produce an avalanche of tears, anytime, anywhere. I really had to rely on God's power. I am also grateful I had a changed heart and a stronger relationship with my Lord and Savior. I had to place more effort in fighting temptations of not allowing my loneliness to accept the wrong people in my life.

Do I pick up where I left off when I was single? Thanks to the Holy Word and the repetition of Psalm 51:10, I learned to trust God. However, I did take advantage of my desires to travel during this season. I traveled to Rome, London, France, New Zealand, Greece, Hawaii, and Australia. The list goes on and the quest to combat loneliness was futile. I was really skeptical about blind dates. One blind date had me sitting in a restaurant, sharing a meal with a man who spent time in prison for robbing a bank. Another date would drink liquor as if it were water. Just when I gave up looking for a companion through blind dating, my last blind date is now my wonderful husband, Harvey. I'm pressing on the upward way.

Urgent Prayers

Charlesetta McCollough

One of my most urgent prayers occurred on December 8, 1968, when I prayed for God to save my life, which was threatened by a rapist on my way to work at 10 p.m. I was accosted, cut, and dragged off a New York street in Brooklyn into an abandoned building and raped. The rapist had already cut me and continued threatening to kill me. I was bleeding profusely as my life flashed before my very eyes. I wondered to myself who would take care of my one-and-a-half-year-old child. Would anyone ever find me in the basement of that abandoned building? That very night, as I prayed in my heart, God showed up and a great peace surrounded me, and my fear was gone just like that. I felt it seemed like God had encircled me in his arms. Suddenly, the rapist told me to leave; I was without any underclothing. I grabbed my coat (winter lime) and fled out to the street half-naked to a firehouse around the corner and was taken to the hospital immediately by the firemen. I can truly say God hears and answers the urgent prayers of the heart. God truly saved my life from a rapist that night.

My mother passed away without any death policy insurance in her name, and I had no way or no money to bury her with or have enough money for a funeral. When the hospital called me and told me my mother was deceased, I was panic-stricken, not only with grief but a financial disaster. How could I afford a funeral for my dear, sweet, loving, kind, wonderful, and beautiful mother? God, my heavenly Father, began to nourish me, calm my fears, soothe my grief, which was almost overwhelming to me. In the meantime, he was preparing the hearts of my coworkers and family members to contribute to me to make funeral arrangements. My mother passed on Wednesday, September 15, 1982. By Monday, September 21st, 1982, I had my mother's funeral.

There is nothing too hard nor impossible for God to bring to pass. My family had very little money but gave what they could; fortunately, I worked for the postal service in Brooklyn, New York, which had thirty-eight post offices. Notices were sent to those post offices requesting donations to help a fellow coworker in need. Some of the workers knew me but most did not, but they kindly contributed very generously toward my mother's funeral. I had always been taught Christian values and faith in God by my godly mother, and God intervened in my urgent and desperate situation. Philippians 4:19 says "But my God shall supply all your need according to his riches in glory by Christ Jesus." And he is super, abundantly above what I needed supplied for me spiritually and financially. To God be the glory.

Love, your friend in Christ, Charlesetta.

I Want Jesus to Walk with Me

Harvey's Response

I was involved in an encounter with a female who hit me on my forehead with a cast-iron frying pan, accusing me of flirting with her woman. The blow to my forehead knocked me out. My grandma tried to stop the bleeding, but she couldn't. I ended up in the emergency room, receiving six stitches. I am wearing the scars to this very day. On another occasion, I had a gun pressed against my throat when a young teenager robbed me of my sneakers, and I had to run about five blocks, barefooted, on a very cold winter night in February 2003. I know the good Lord had his hands on me. During this period of time, my lifestyle placed me in too many perilous situations, where my life was threatened. Oh, how I love Jesus.

My financial association with Charlesetta's testimony was collecting funds for my sister's funeral. Miccie passed away suddenly without an insurance policy. Our family pulled together to give my sister a decent funeral. I had to give my whole check for this purpose, which included my money for rent. I can truly say that God is a great provider, and I am truly grateful he allowed the funeral to meet the family's traditions during our bereavement.

Never Could Have Made It

Margaret's Response

I had a strong association with Charlesetta's testimony. I lived in New York for thirty-five years, and I am well aware of the crimes that have taken place. I was a victim of a very serious mugging. Two teenage boys followed me from the subway station as I was going home at 11:00 p.m. I was returning home from a trip to Virginia. My house was two blocks away from the subway station, but the first block was surrounded with overgrown shrubbery. I didn't realize that the boys were following me. I was four doors away from my house when one of the boys caught up with me and knocked me to the ground. He was brandishing a gun as they pulled my suitcase and purse. I screamed for help only once because they threatened to shoot me if I screamed again, so I followed directions in exchange for my life. No neighbors responded to my scream until the boys kicked me and ran away with my belongings. At that point, a neighbor came out, asked me what was wrong. The police were called, and the next day I spent an hour at the police station, looking at photos of criminals. I failed to recognize either attacker; unfortunately, that was the end of that story.

Another story where I remembered experiencing extreme fear took place in Baltimore. I was in the fifth grade, and my nana purchased a house for my family to live in along with my Uncle Buddy and his family. We were the first Black family on Gwynn Avenue. We were received in the neighborhood with all sorts of rejections. We had to have the police guard our house for twenty days because some unfriendly neighbors threw rocks and stones through our windows. My fears intensified after the police completed their assignment to guard our house. My brother, Donald, and I were chased by several white boys with dogs as we walked to school. A white boy spit in my face outside the neighborhood store. We were called "n——" and "black monkeys." We received vulgar threats of what would happen to us if we didn't move out of that neighborhood. Mother invested prayers for peace and security. Those prayers were answered when other Black families moved on the block; harassment ceased, and we were able to stay in our home.

The second part of her testimony was even closely related to a financial situation I had in preparing and paying for Nana's funeral in 2000. Nana had always been secretive about her life and personal business. When I received the news that Nana had passed, I immediately fell to my knees and asked the Lord to help me. At this time, there were five grandchildren to assume the financial responsibilities. Nana's nieces and nephews didn't know of any insurance policies that Nana may have left with her sister. My prayers were answered the day before the funeral. My cousin Alva found a policy for Nana. Hallelujah, Hallelujah, God answered my prayers.

Learning to Pray Again

Cynthia Ford

All my life, I prayed every day, then I had a devastating loss in my life, and I questioned God why this happened to me. I always pray when things are good and bad. I lost the feeling of prayer, but that bothered me. I went to a retreat and one of the subjects was *learning how* to *pray*, and a strange lady sat beside me. When it was time to pray, she held my hand and pulled me into the aisle and started to pray for me. I could feel her spirit. I fell on my knees and started to pray. It had been three months since I said a prayer. I was so uplifted and free. This happened twenty-four years Ago, and through the years I have learned not to give up on God because he's always there no matter what you're going through. He will deliver you. We want things the way we perceive them, but that's not God's way. God has taught me to be patient and wait on him. Later I found out the strange lady who prayed for me was an evangelist. She said God pointed me out to her, and that's why she sat beside me. You never know what's in store for you. I created two prayers from verses of the Bible and other spiritual pamphlets. Start the day with God, end your day with prayer.

Start the Day with God

This is the day that the Lord has made, and I will rejoice and be glad in it. I start every day with God by speaking life, health, strength, and vitality into my body because I know God's healing power is at work within me. The nature and life of God are resident in my body, driving out all manner of sickness, disease, and worry. I refuse to get stressed out; I refuse to worry or be anxious. I stand firm and fearless in my faith. Weakness, tiredness, and weariness, I command you to get out of my body. I can do all things through Christ who strengthens me because God is for me, God is with me, and God is in me. I will not fear any obstacles or difficulties that might come my way. I will not weaken or cave in because God is with me, and I can conquer anything. I will never, never, never quit; I am strong in the Lord and the power of his might. His Word says that by Jesus stripes, I am healed and have been redeemed. I believe the Word of God above anything that I think, feel, or see. In the name of Jesus.

Amen! Amen! Amen!

End Your Day with Prayer

The spirit of the Lord is on me. He quickens me and gives me strength. In him I find rest, comfort, and peace. Even in the midst of the storms of life, I am calm, cool, and collected because my mind is focused on Jesus. He keeps me in perfect peace. I have confidence in God's word; I choose not to worry or be anxious about anything. I will not allow myself to be fearful and troubled about any circumstance in my life. I have released my faith. I have received my healing according to the promise of his word, and now all that's left for me to do is rest. My God has promised to give his beloved sweet sleep. Therefore, I will receive a full night's sleep every night, and I fully expect to wake up in the morning refreshed, revitalized, and raring to go. Thank you, Jesus, for this day, yesterday, and tomorrow. I give you praise and honor. In the name of Jesus. Amen! Amen! Amen! Amen!

"Where thou liest down, thou shall not be afraid: Yea, thou shalt lie down, and thy sleep shall be sweet" (Proverbs 3:24).

I Need Thee

Harvey's Reflection

My reflection from Cynthia's testimony comes from an incident in prison that I will always remember. Every Thursday someone from a clergy status would visit the prison to deliver an inspiring word from the Bible. One Thursday, a white clergyman came to our block and stood on the outside of our cell. As he was trying to accomplish his mission, his audience of inmates appeared to have rejected what he was saying. The inmates immediately threw out vulgarities, objects containing urine, papers, spit, and anything they could throw through the bars. The clergyman stood firm and proceeded with his mission. I didn't join this unwarranted response. As a matter of fact, I pleaded to them to stop. I was seriously impressed and inspired by the strength of this man. He didn't stop until his mission was fulfilled. I approached him and asked him if he would pray for me. He responded instantly and he prayed.

I harbored his image, standing strong. I was inspired to the point that I decided I wanted to possess that type of strength. So I replaced playing spades and watching TV with praying and Bible reading. Two or three of my inmates observed my newly adopted routine, and they came to my bunk asking questions and sharing opinions, Unintentionally, Harvey's Bible study was created. Surprisingly, the group continued to grow. I had trouble pronouncing a lot of the words, but I allowed the Holy Spirit to have his way.

God showed up at every meeting, every day, around my bunk for several weeks. Satan tried intruding into some of our meetings.

We prayed and can testify; we, a group of seven inmates, witnessed manifestations of invested prayers. One time, an inmate objected to our meeting and banged on a metal trash can, singing, yelling, and making disruptive noises. I approached him with my Bible in my hand. I asked him to stop and said a short prayer. Minutes later he stopped, and we noticed the entire dorm became quiet. We continued our study in peace. My reflection is, God places people in your life to help make a change or to restore.

I Have Decided to Follow Jesus

Margaret Reflects

I had attended the same retreat Cynthia mentioned in her testimony. I recalled the spiritual growth we impounded from the experiences we shared from that retreat. Cynthia and I have been friends since the seventh grade. We declared ourselves as BFFs, best friends forever. My thoughts traveled to my sphere of influence. My thoughts were not judgmental, but they were based on how various friends affected my life. I realized all of us need people in our life. I remember and categorize friends who had a positive affect and friends who had a negative effect. My sphere of influence had a great impact on my decision-making, as well as being a factor in the development of a few personal insecurities. However, the choice in the crisis was mine to make.

I wish I could reveal that I included God in all my decision-making, but I didn't. There was a time when I chose to become overly friendly with a mutual acquaintance of my first husband and me. It was confirmed to me that Robert was having an affair with another woman, so that justified my overfriendly reactions toward my new temptation. I thought about the hurt my father caused my mother, and I swore I wouldn't allow a man to cheat and hurt me the same way. At that time, I had a revengeful spirit and an unforgiving heart. Thank God for my spiritual growth; he changed my heart and renewed my spirit. Robert and I had the opportunity to discuss our adulterous transgressions toward each other and forgive each other before he passed away. Yes, we prayed for God's forgiveness.

Berthina Burns's Testimony

Berthina Burns

As of 2021, I rejoice at knowing that I'm cancer-free. Eight years ago, I discovered a lump in the right armpit of my arm while taking a shower. I postponed going to the doctors immediately due to having to go to Pennsylvania to attend to my daughter. On my return home, I went to the doctor and the doctor became alarmed by what she discovered and informed my oldest daughter, who accompanied me to my appointment. Within a few days of my initial week after appointment, the doctor sent me in for a biopsy. I was given my diagnosis of breast cancer.

After coming home from the appointment, I can remember being overwhelmed with fear and anxiety—fear that led me into praying to God filled with tears, begging him to heal my body, and in a quiet, still voice that I had never heard before and long to hear again, I heard the Lord say, "It's done, I have already healed you." For the first time during my first discovery of this lump, I was able to rest. I must have dozed asleep, but I remember feeling a peace and comfort that is still to this day indescribable.

Still having to go through the process of CT scans and mammograms, I felt totally overwhelmed but remembered what God had spoken to me. The oncologist couldn't find a trace of cancer but, wanting to lean on the side of caution, they advised me to have thirteen lymph nodes removed under my arm, followed up by chemotherapy for a period of six months.

Chemotherapy treatments consisted of two appointments every altering week and one treatment in between. Six months of chemotherapy treatments would be followed by radiation to shrink any possible mass for three months, and then surgery.

The first day of chemotherapy was not as bad, but day two was a nightmare. I mustered up enough energy for my next round. As a result of month-long chemotherapy, my hair had started to fall out. I knew immediately that I was not going to go through this process, and this would be something that I would have the power over. I went right to the bathroom, grabbed my husband's clippers, and shaved all my hair off. That would settle it, I shaved it, cancer didn't take it.

Six weeks of radiation at one appointment a week. Radiation was kinder to me than chemotherapy; with the loss of appetite, gingersnaps became my go-to snack. Radiation caused me to faint regularly, but thank God for my husband and granddaughter for being there to help me. I could feel the fainting coming on the same days; I was able to sit and on other days found the floor to catch me. I would have never imagined in a thousand years having to fight such a fight, but I am thankful for the grace of God that brought me through. I didn't always feel good, but I found happiness in each day knowing what the Lord had promised me. I knew it was only the Lord who had spoken those words to me because it was a voice that I had never heard before; it was a feeling that I have never experienced before. To this day I still have not heard that voice again, but it was more than enough to get me through my biggest adversary and to carry me through until this very day. I had experienced the audible voice of God; I had experienced his glory.

After the surgery, chemotherapy, and radiation, my healing was a strength process—building up my energy, strengthening my arm, and building my body back up. I had to physically go through the motion. God had healed me months ago; my body had to match my spirit. My outward man had to catch up with what the Lord had already done for me the night he spoke to me. My testimony and advice to others is to believe the report of the Lord. Hold on and walk out what God said. He may not speak to you in an audible voice, but trust that when you need him, he'll answer and do exactly what he said he will do.

Won't God Do It?

Margaret's Response

I sincerely applaud, glorify, and rejoice with Sister Burns for her blessings as a cancer survivor. I immediately thought of the cancer victims in my family; my father and my sister. The good Lord took them home. I will never forget, July 27, 1987; my Uncle Milton called me to inform me of his care—training. He volunteered to be the caregiver upon Daddy's release from his three-week stay in the hospital. Uncle Milton lived in Baltimore, and I lived in New York. The call came in at 10:28 saying my father would be released the next morning. Twenty minutes later, Uncle Milton called to say my father died ten minutes ago. My father had lung cancer, diabetes, amputation of his right leg, and complications from a serious stroke.

My sister, Mildred, was diagnosed on August 29, 2009, with stage 3 lung cancer. She passed away on January 23, 2012. Mildred was on hospice status for twelve weeks. She lost all of her hair, even her eyebrows. So many days and nights, I witnessed her suffering with agonizing pain. Those episodes of pain-bearing made me feel helpless yet hopeful. Every single day of those twelve weeks was an answer to an invested prayer; God allowed her to see another day. My rejoicing involved seeing how she turned her life over to Jesus before she died. She joined church and was re-baptized, confessing her restoration and intentions to serve our risen Savior. Needless to think, I was very grateful that she shared her children and even allowed Robert and me to legally adopt her first child, Erica. I will never forget a very frightful experience during Mildred's conquest; the cancer had metastasized to her brain. Mildred abruptly interrupted our conversation on our children with a question: "Is David, our baby brother, dead or alive?" I was stunned. When I told her he was dead, she jumped up and banged the television with her fist. David died in 1974 and we were in 2012. So Berthina has a genuine testimony; she survived cancer. Won't God do it?

Joyful, Joyful, We Adore Thee

Harvey's Response

As far as I know, we haven't had any family members with cancer. I remembered an occasion in prison during one of our Bible study sessions. An inmate who appeared confused about his choice of worshipping faith came to my bunk, visibly upset, asking for prayer for his grandma. He had just received a call that she was dying from cancer in the hospital. I asked him three questions: Do you believe in Jesus? Do you believe he can heal your grandmother? Do you believe in prayer? His answers were yes, yes, and yes. So each of the six men in attendance took turns praying for the grandmother, including the inmate himself, and I said the last prayer. The next night the inmate returned to my bunk, exclaiming joyfully, "She is healed!" The last test showed no cancer. She was coming home. He said I did it, but I immediately corrected him, reassuring him that it was God. I took no credit nor did any of the participants for the miracle. All of us invested prayers.

Trust and Believe: Prayer Changes Things

Peggy Lawrence

I've always trusted and believe in Christ, and I also have prayed. But through my bad experience, what I'm about to reveal is the true realization that prayer changes things if you only trust and believe.

I had been employed with the city of New York Board of Education for two years and had received two satisfactory year-ending ratings thus far. I was in my third year of employment at that time; March of that year began my journey through hell. The principal who had received principalship of MS180 (ironically, my old alma mater) came from another school in the building down from MS180 as the new principal. Now some of the things I can say are (1) I take pride in whatever I do; (2) if I'm not sick, I come to work and be on time; (3) I've never been one to sit around waiting to be told what to do. If I see something not in order, I put it in order. I like to work, enjoy my job and stay busy. With that being said, I don't know what it was about me that this principal didn't like. To make a long story short, she began to task me and blame me for things that weren't my job. True, at that time, I was the pupil account secretary (for students), and I had a lot of things to stay on top of where they were concerned. But one thing that was out of my control was "making the parents stay on top of their child's immunization." This reflected a red flag on the school but was also pointed at the pupil accounting secretary. For a school to receive 100 percent in immunization was a good thing.

All I could do was make calls, send letters, and during parent/teacher conference, I would confront the parents of their child's immunization status, in hopes of them adhering to the severity of this information being updated. This principal would give me an assignment to type something, then give to the school aide to retype and confront me that I typed it wrong. She did not afford me the opportunity to work on weekends and make extra money as she did the payroll secretary. At the year's end, she gave me an unsatisfactory rating with discontinuance of service. Again, she was the principal from March of that year to June. In my numbness, I had refused to sign the document as she did not know how to complete the form; she made x's on everything except my attire and attendance, and she didn't make any comments. After the deadline to give me this document had passed and she realized she did it wrong, she submitted to me another rating sheet with checkmarks and comments. I was stunned.

The union prep had advised me how to file a claim to rebut this action, and I would have to meet with an arbitrator. I was worried, stressed, and one day as I was on my way to a hearing regarding this situation, I began to break into cold sweat, go out of breath, and I immediately got off the train. I went to the token booth and asked the worker to call an ambulance for me as I felt I was having a heart attack. She called, the ambulance arrived, and the needle on the monitor went haywire. The EMT said they were taking me to the nearest hospital. I stated that I was a veteran and wanted to go to the VA hospital. But I would not have made it. Was I on my way to dying? I was hospitalized for four days and had to endure a stressed test. This was my first knowledge that stress could kill you. I pulled through because I trusted, believed, and prayed. The union rep I had was no good use to me. It appeared to me that she was on the side of the enemy. She spoke of nothing in my defense.

During July and August, I took the chance and reapplied for another school for September of that year; I was accepted. But the U-rating followed me to that school, and I had to leave and I was told that there was something wrong with my secretary school license. So I began to pray and look to the hills. I found peace in Psalms 27,

31, 34, 37, 40, and 55. I prayed diligently and sincerely. Suddenly, I began to get calls to substitute. I went from one school to the next. I received an assignment that was a month long, under the heading of F-status, which was more money. I continued to work, and I continued to pray. On top of that, I received a call from a woman whom I had only spoken to on the phone as she was a district office person who dealt with school secretaries. We have never met, and she said she had an assignment that was temporary, which could be long term. Did I want it? I said, "Thank you, Jesus," took the address, and drove to the school so as not to be late the next day. This was in September or October, I think, and I got the job. Once again, I came to work, did my job and above, and moved about with professionalism and thoroughness as usual. The principal there, Dr. Coye (I'll never forget him as he was truly a good and kind man who gave me a chance), hired me that November, and I was placed back in the school system. There were a few stumbling blocks along the way, but I continue to pray and was able to retire with twenty-two years of service from the city of New York. Prayer changes things if you only trust and believe.

Prayerfully submitted by Sister Peggy Ann Lawrence
Riverview, Florida 33578

Blessed Assurance

Margaret's Reflections

I came so close to losing my teacher's license when I tapped a student on his leg with a plastic bat. My intention was to get him to take his place in line. I know it was only a tap despite my feelings of losing patience with him. When I tapped him on his right leg, he ran down the hall. As he ran, his mother was walking through the door of the school. After he saw his mother, he started to cry and scream that I hurt him. I went through the chain of investigation, praying each step of the way. I resumed my position as a sixth-grade teacher for emotionally disturbed students. God answered my invested prayers.

Another occasion of Satan interfering on my job was when I was an assistant director of an after-school program of John Edward Bruce Day Care Center. I actually took a week off, pretending I was sick. I went on a train trip with Erica to Disney World. Someone told the director what I had done. I was wrong, but I had paid for the trip months ahead. I had also requested the time, but the director failed to write it on the calendar. I won my case with the board and God's mercy. I was blessed with six months of probation. I had a doctor's note and the person who told the director didn't appear for the investigation meeting. I believe this incident was based on personality conflict between the director and me.

He's Got the Whole World in His Hands

Harvey's Reactions

Although Peggy's testimony didn't have any indication of racism, I thought of an incident I experienced at the workplace where I had to quit due to a conflict of values. I worked for a white man who constantly expressed racism in conversations. I didn't pay attention during the first five years, but in my sixth year, we talked frequently. He said he didn't agree with Black people living in the same neighborhood with white people. He also said he won't work for Blacks; they work for him. I asked him if he was a racist and he proudly said yes, he was a racist. Once he asked me to mow his lawn and he only wanted the back lawn done, and I had to enter his house from the back door. Black workers had to sit in a cage-like section of his van. There were increasing incidents and evidence of his racism. I had to quit.

Another unfair event toward me was in drug court. I was accused of breaking a girl's anonymity. She told the clinicians I discussed her status and activities with her boyfriend. I told them we talked, and he asked me what was going on with his girl in drug court. I told him I wasn't allowed to say anything about anybody there. One of the clinicians asked the girl for her boyfriend's phone number. They called him and asked what he and I discussed. He told them exactly what I told them. She lied, and I could have gone to jail for the accusation.

Prayer Still Works

Jo-Ann Moore

Praise the Lord! I just want to take this time to give God the honor, the glory, and the praise for his goodness and his mercy toward me, his humble servant and daughter. I want to spend this moment sharing with you the goodness of God in my life as I give my testimony of how he answers prayer. Prayer is real, and God hears an answered prayer daily. The moment that I want to share with you happened in December of 2015 when, just like his servant Job, the enemy attacked my body with sickness. This is just one of the many circumstances that he bought me through.

I recall the times that I would be standing in the mirror, combing my hair, and my hands would begin to cramp up, and my fingers would begin to curl up, making it difficult to open my hands. I had to use one curled-up hand to push the fingers of the opposite hand open. Moments later, my legs began to get cramps in the calf muscles. I, just as many others do, began to self-diagnose my problems. I thought maybe this was happening because I had not enough bananas for potassium. I needed to stretch my muscles and exercise and drink more water. My thinking was if I did those things, I would be okay, so that is what I attempted to do. For two weeks, problems began to reoccur.

My bedroom was in the basement of my home, and the only bathroom in the house was on the second floor. As I climbed the stairs to the top floor, I felt more winded than usual by the time I reached the second floor. I called and I talked to my doctor about it, and he asked me if I had chest pains and a water intake, and he suggested that I call him if the problems continued after a week. I did not think much about my symptoms for the next few days until a reoccurrence took place. This time was different. I was driving my grandkids to school one afternoon, and my chest began to hurt a little and feel a bit tight. While in my car, I called my doctor, and I explained to the doctor how I was feeling. He informed me that I needed to get my hands on some aspirin and go to the emergency room. I explained to him that I had young children in my car who needed to be dropped off at afternoon pre-K, and I could not just stop what I was doing because there was no one to care of them, so he told me to take an aspirin as soon as I could and get to the hospital right away.

I did what he said, but I did not go straight to the emergency room that day; I went later that evening, only to find the emergency room super crowded. I texted my daughters to inform them of my whereabouts after being rushed to the triage area for an EKG and a barrage of questions. I was sent into the waiting area where I sat conversing on my cell phone. After four or five hours of waiting, my patients grew weary, and I gave back the pager that the triage nurse had given me and told her that I was leaving. Instead of going to another hospital, I went back home. I was not feeling terrible, and my breathing had gotten better, so it seemed. But most of all, I just wanted to go home and get into my bed to relax—that is just what I did. I took the aspirin as recommended by the physician, curled up in my pajamas, watched a bit of television while still on the telephone, and eventually said my prayers, especially for healing and God's protection for myself and my loved ones, and I drifted off to sleep (while praying, I may add.)

A little after midnight, I was startled by the phone ringing. It was the doctor from the emergency room. She did not ask how I was feeling at that moment, but she just told me of the reason of my visit to the ER, as if I did not already know why I was there, and told me that she advised me to come back that night. Well, stubborn me asked her a few questions. "Is the emergency room still crowded?" Her reply, "Yes." "Can you assure me that I will be taken to the back

Invested Prayers

to be seen when I get there?" Her reply, "No," My response was "I appreciate your concern, I can come back tomorrow," and I hung up the phone. I did go back the next day after I took my granddaughter to afternoon pre-K. It was less crowded, and I did not have a long wait after being triaged before I was taken to a room in the back. It was not until then, while I was lying on that gurney, that I realized that God is a prayer answered for even those of us who are stubborn and hardheaded.

For weeks, my daughters had been saying, "Mommy, you need to go to the hospital or your doctor's office to get checked out." But I didn't feel the urgency or the severity of my health issues. I just did not feel sick, I felt more stressed out than anything. Anyway, God knows what is going to happen even before it ever happens. He heard my prayers, and he answered them. After walking into that emergency room with my own strength, by the time I got into the hospital gown and finished explaining my symptoms to the nurse, I felt like I was losing power. That loss became my reality after I climbed off the gurney to go to the ladies' room. I had been lying down on the gurney in an inclined position for a little while after the nurse had hooked me up with the IV drip. The nurse's station was right outside of my room, and the restroom was about ten to fifteen feet across the hall from my room. Just in that short walk to and from the restroom, my breathing became more rapid, and the more the fluids that were being pumped into my veins, the more I had to use the restroom. Still lying in bed on an inclined angle, my daughter called and wanted to come to the hospital with me, but I insisted that I was all right, it was not necessary for them to come with the small children who are my grandbabies. I called my pastor, who is also my brother, and we had prayed together and hung up. I got up again to use the bathroom, pushing the IV pole with me. I noticed a few doctors standing in the hall, talking a few doors down from my room, but more than that, I felt my struggle with breathing grow stronger.

By the time I finished in the restroom and walked back into my room, I was breathing as if I had just run a marathon. The doctors that I saw in the hallway just so happened to be coming to see me, and they saw the difference in my breathing pattern going into the restroom and a greater difference coming back out. After I climbed back into bed, I looked at the picture of my daughters on my phone and said to God, "Lord, I am not afraid to die because I know that I will be with you in heaven. But what I do not know is if these three daughters that you gave to me will be able handle it. Bless them and keep them, Jesus." An x-ray technician knocked on the door and brought the x-ray machine with him to take x-rays of my chest. He sat my bed up into a full upright position, and I thought that I was going to die. I could not breathe, and I could barely get the words out to tell him to hurry up and finish because I could not breathe.

After the doctors checked the x-ray film, they sent me to get a CAT scan with dye because nothing showed up on the x-ray. My youngest daughter called to check up on me, and I told her what had transpired since we last spoke. She too is a minister, and she began to minister to me. She said, "Mommy, you are always helping everybody else, and you are always praying for and ministering to everybody else. Now, it is your turn to be ministered to." She added, "People believe in doctors and scientists, but we believe in Jesus!" After those words, every word that followed was a blur. When she was finished, a single tear rolled from my left eye. I had peace in my soul and fear never overcame me throughout the whole ordeal, and just after she hung up the phone, those same three doctors that I saw in the hall came into my room. The one closest to me took the tip of the sheet that was covering me and dabbed the one tear from the corner of my eye and said to me, "You don't have to cry, we know what is happening to you now."

He began to explain to me that both of my lungs were filling up with blood clots, but at that moment, they knew how to stop the clots from continuing to form. Another doctor said, "I know that you are saved because only God could have kept me from death." The third doctor said, "You don't know how sick you are, if you had not come into the hospital when you did, you would not be alive tomorrow." This is my testimony of God's grace, mercy, and favor in my life. I prayed, my pastor prayed, my daughter prayed for me and with me, and God knows who prayed for me without my knowledge. The blessing is, he answered every prayer, and I am profoundly

Invested Prayers

grateful to him and all who pray for me then and now. The Bible says in the book of James 5:16, "Confess your faults one to another, and pray for one for another, that you may be healed. The effectual fervent prayer of a righteous man avails much" (KJV). Please believe me, prayer changes things, be encouraged. God has not forgotten about you. He knows what you are faced with, and he will see you through.

Keep the faith, God still answers prayer.
God bless you!

He's a Healer

Harvey's Response

I can truly say amen, amen, and amen again to JoAnn's testimony. As previously stated, God has healed me physically from all of my surgeries despite my current disability status. God has allowed me to complete many home-repair jobs as needed income for our budget, but when I think a little deeper, I realize his mercies exceeded physical healings. He has healed me with my intellectual abilities. I am learning things I should have learned in high school when I thought being the class clown was more important. My vocabulary has increased. I hate writing because I had problems spelling, but God has shown me ways to attack the problem, and now I can write with more confidence. He has healed me in my development of the fruit of the Spirit (Gelatin 5:22–23), especially my temper and my impulsiveness to fight with my fist to solve a problem or deal with a difficult person. This has changed because I have changed. Let God arise and my enemies be scattered.

Great Is Thy faithfulness

Margaret's Response

Fear was my association with JoAnn's testimony. I was rushed to the intensive care unit during a medical procedure to insert a stent in my right leg. A blood clot was revealed, and the procedure was interrupted. All types of IVs were administered. Just knowing I was in that unit nearly ushered me into a panic mode. Was I going to die? I realized that I was fearful and ready to panic. When I calmed down, I remembered to invest a prayer for the medicine to work and dissolve the blood clot before it traveled to my heart. I was grateful God heard my prayers. I had to include the request that God would also strengthen my faith, help me to release the fear I was experiencing. I had to regroup and claim my belief that God was able to deliver me. I recited the twenty-third psalm over and over again until I could rest in knowing that God is always in control. I had to trust God and place my mind in a position to accept his will for my life.

My husband, Harvey, and my daughter, Erica, were at my bedside. Most of all, God was with me. For a moment, I allowed fear to taunt me. Satan is a liar; according to John 8:44, Satan is the father of liars. I also thought about another time I experienced fear when my sister, Mildred, was changing her mind about allowing my first husband, Robert, and I to adopt her baby girl. Thank God the adoption was successful! Four years later, Erica was struck with life-threatening meningitis. I had to face this problem almost alone because Robert and I were separated at that time. He was supportive in his own way, but he wrongfully blamed me for causing this misfortune.

Someone would have to be at Erica's bedside continuously to make sure her IV attachments wouldn't be pulled out of her arm. Mildred left Baltimore to help. Within six hours of Mildred's arrival, she fell ill and had to go to the emergency room. Thank God I learned how to exercise my faith without doubting and fearing. Great is his faithfulness.

I Believe in Prayer

Eric Smith

From the age of either eleven or twelve, I started experimenting with smoking, drinking, and drugs, which led to criminal activities that sentenced me to twenty years in prison at the age of sixteen, with parole after nine years and nine months. I had abandoned my faith in God and belief in the power of prayer.

Upon release from prison, I was back behind bars after only seven months free. Within two weeks of my arrest, I suffered a brain hemorrhage that caused sight loss in both eyes' left peripheral vision. I also experienced equilibrium loss and acquired a seizure disorder. Prior to my diagnosis of an occipital brain aneurysm, I laid in a pre-trial jail cell and cried, pleading for medical attention but to no avail.

Finally, while curried up in a fetal position in excruciating pain, I fervently prayed to God to take away my pain and suffering. The medical department finally considered the possible risk to take my life, and I was transported to the ICU. I beseeched my God to save my life, and God answered my prayers with a resounding explanation: "You are going to be all right!"

Now, thirty-four years later, I pray ceaselessly for God to protect us all in his infinite wisdom. Prayer reminds me that we worry too much, not remembering the majesty of God. There is nothing that exists that is not known of and by God, and there is no path that we take in life that cannot be corrected.

In that same time frame, I experienced a warm, overwhelming flush throughout my body and an immense flow of tears of exonerating joy, the likes of which I'd never felt before and never experienced again afterward. It is said by some to have been the indwelling of the Holy Spirit.

For me, the solemn oath faith comes through incessant prayer.

Call Him Up and Tell Him What You Want

Harvey's Response

There are two things I can associate my life's story with Eric's testimony; I have experienced prison life, and I have experienced excruciating pain. When I was working at the commissary at Langley Air Force Base, I was pulling a pilot jack full of products. My coworker stopped pushing. I thought I could pull it myself, but the load threw me to the floor. They had to call the ambulance. I was diagnosed with a pinched nerve in my neck. I had to have surgery, cutting out the bone spurs and inserting a metal cage in my neck. I had to have a second surgery because a screw came loose in my neck from the first surgery. A few years later, I had to have back surgery due to degenerative arthritis. Following this surgery, I had to have another back surgery in 2018, replacing the original rods in my back. Recuperation was slow and very, very painful. I invested a lot of prayers for healing. The loneliness and the absence of family and friends seem to make the pain more excruciating, but knowing Jesus and remembering that I could go to him in prayer got me relief and healing. I would have to acknowledge my two friends, Kelvin and Ann, who helped when they could.

Trust and Obey for There Is No Other Way to Be Happy in Jesus

Margaret's Response

My immediate reactions went to the benefits of obedience and the consequences of disobedience. I remembered receiving my first spanking from my mother when I was in the second grade; I came home about fifteen minutes late. My mother was worried. She scolded me, promising to spank me if I went to the store before coming home late again. I made a promise not to go to the store. The very next day my classmate convinced me that we could run to the store and run home in time, so we tried. We met my mother halfway home. Mom kept her promise after she survived an oncoming asthma attack, she used the strap to spank me three times. I remembered the commandment I was taught in Sunday school from Exodus 20:12: "Honor thy father and thy mother."

In my late teenage years (around nineteen), I came very close to being arrested. I was on a date with a guy who drank too much at a party. I took the keys from him and drove his car. He and I argued as I was driving with a learning permit. I made a wrong turn on a popular street. I had not started my exploration into alcohol. As I tried to correct the mistake and turn the vehicle in the right direction, police showed up. I explained to the officer why I was driving. He gave me a ticket. My grandmother went to court with me. The judge gave me a fine of $160.00, and I only had $50.00. My grandmother asked if she could be excused for a moment. She said she would come back with the money. I had to have the money or spend time in jail. My grandmother went to the restroom and pulled the balance of the fine from the money covered in a sock from her bosom. Grandma told me before the date that I shouldn't date him because we knew he drank alcohol. I was close to going to jail because I didn't listen. I have made plenty of bad decisions pertaining to involvement with people, underestimating or overestimating. One of the observations my mother expressed to me was how proud of me she was that I had graduated from high school, but she had real concerns with my selection of friends. I had tendencies to love hard and was sincerely expecting to receive the return of the same emotions.

I Know the Plans I Have for You

Helen Dixon Moore

> "For I know the plans I have for you," declares the Lord, "plans to prosper you and not to harm you, plans to give you hope and a future."
>
> —Jeremiah 29:11 (NIV)

Years ago, when I was growing up in Newport News, Virginia, during my elementary and high school days, my family lived on a street which had a drugstore on the corner. It sold everything a kid could ever want when it came to sweet treats and snacks and, believe it or not, twenty-five cents—or a quarter—went a long way in those days; with it you could buy a bag of potato chips (five cents), a soft drink (five cents), an ice cream treat (five cents), a candy bar (five cents), which costs about a dollar today, and then an assortment of candy for a penny apiece or butter cookies which were two for a penny. So, as you can see, twenty-five cents automatically put you in kid heaven, and I walked by that drugstore twice a day, to and from the elementary school and, later, that same corner was my high school bus stop.

Not only was the drugstore on the corner of my street, but the church was right across the street where we were members; I attended faithfully until I went away to college. Miss Parker, who also lived across the street, always had me go to the drugstore for her, and she would pay me three cents or sometimes five cents. So, from time to time, I had a little stash of cash.

Then one day, when I was in sixth grade, I had money, which I decided to spend at the drugstore. But as I was on my way, I suddenly stopped and declared aloud that I was not going to spend the money at the store but instead put it in the offering plate at church. My prayer was for God to bless me with a good job. Today I can say, without any equivocation whatsoever, that he honored the seed I sowed and the prayer I prayed that day as a child.

When I look back over my life from that moment, it was crystal clear to me that God had orchestrated things and events in my life. After graduating as valedictorian of my high school class, I attended Fisk University, majoring in economics. By April of my senior year, I had several job offers from corporate America and had officially accepted a job at Westinghouse in Pittsburgh, Pennsylvania, and had even made plans in that regard. However, about two weeks prior to commencement, at the proverbial "eleventh hour," I received an offer from the Office of the Secretary of Defense, at the Pentagon, to be an executive trainee in its management intern program—a position I did not seek, did not apply for, and for which I was never interviewed. I wrote a kind letter to Westinghouse reversing my acceptance and instead went on to work at the Pentagon. So with that, I began my professional federal government career as a grade GS-7 program analyst and retired thirty-three years later as chief of my agency's management information team at the GS-15 grade level with a six-figure salary. For me, God did that thing.

"And the Lord appointed a set time, saying, "Tomorrow the Lord shall do this thing in the land." And the Lord did that thing (Exodus 9:5–6 KJV).

Standing on the Promises of Christ, My King

Margaret's Response

My reflections pertaining to Helen's testimony took me back to a career history. I was given the title and position of assistant director of John Edward Bruce Day Care Center in Brooklyn, New York, on June 24, 1975. I was offered the position without actually applying for the position. At last, someone recognized my capabilities when I doubted myself. Thank you, Jesus, for the hidden blessing; however, the beginning of her testimony gave birth to a present-day challenge I'm experiencing. As she expressed various changes she witnessed, my challenge is transitioning from middle-age to senior status: losing hair; losing teeth; shrinking height; weakening hearing, vision, and mobility. Waking up with a new pain almost daily and frequently forgetting things, I am learning to be grateful for these conditions, and I am learning to accept these conditions, changing what I can change and using God-given wisdom to accept what I cannot change. I have to invest in the prayer of serenity frequently.

Prayer of Serenity

God, grant me the serenity to accept the things I cannot change, the courage to change the things I can, and the wisdom to know the difference.

Living the Life God Has Planned for Me

Harvey's Response

I experienced enough of life to realize that I can only make changes in my life if I, Harvey Mears, seek the Lord. My destructive behavior became scary, boring, and downright stagnant. The women became more deceiving and the drugs became more addictive and expensive. I recall buying some crack and discovering it was a mixture of sheet rock, nuts, and baking soda. I returned to the dealer with a baseball bat in my hand and the intentions of beating the daylights out of him. I was distracted by a man on a telephone pole telling me, "Man, don't do it." This distraction made me stop and think of the consequences of harming the dealer. I went back home, angry but calm.

When I told this story in a meeting, I received a lot of attention. Addicts appeared to be actively listening and responding with questions and comments. I always knew I had a big mouth, and I was very argumentative. There came a time when I decided to exchange my fist-fighting for tongue lashing. If someone disrespected me, I responded brutally and disrespectfully. I am working on changing, thank God; I am better than I used to be.

Today I use my experience-sharing to encourage the addicts who are seeking recovery from drug addiction. I discovered the importance of sharing, praying, and testifying—to God be the glory. I am very grateful for the gift of bearing witness to some of life's issues, the gift to encourage and help people in need of help. I have a deep willingness to reflect God in my life and my renewed intentions to serve God with all of my heart, for the rest of my life, with the grace and mercies of my Lord.

A Ninety-Four-Year-Old's Prayers

Carolyn Chester

To observe a man who has read books the size of yellow pages but never read the Bible is amazing. He was noted in my story of "three strikes, you're out," so he had firsthand experience of my relationship with God. When I was traveling home after walking the streets alone at night from the train station, he was alarmed about my safety.

"How are you?" He paused with worries and frustration, and I said to him "Pray." I could hear the astonishment in his voice as he paused again, and I hung up the phone.

I arrived home safely, and as I was pushing the buttons on the elevator, he called and I asked him if he prayed for me…another pause and he said yes, his prayers were answered. "I am coming up to your house now," he said.

"Okay," I replied, and I shared my events of my day and plans for tomorrow.

"You were lucky that you had another key."

"No, no," I explained to him. "That is an example of the relationship I have with God."

I left him alone as I got myself ready for bed, and I came in the room where he was sitting and saw this.

Enormous hands embrace together with eyes close, and there were expressions on his face. My first I thought was I was sleeping, but as I watched a little longer, he was praying. I wanted to take a picture, but my phone was near where he was sitting. I asked after disturbing him as to what he was doing and he said yes.

Prayers of a ninety-four-year-old man are priceless. One day I pray he will believe in who is listening and answering those prayers.

Pray for Me

Harvey's Response

Carolyn's testimony made me think of an interview I had with a lady from drug court. My lawyer recommended drug court as opposed to a four-year sentence given by the judge. I was asked why I wanted to get in the program. I told her that God has changed me, and I needed the help the drug court could provide. She firmly shouted, "Do not come into drug court with that religious stuff!" I won't deny him, no, never. I am so glad I have Jesus and he's enough. I will take him everywhere I go. I didn't expect that the drug court would accept me, but they did. There were many sessions and opportunities for me to express my personal relationship with God. He allowed me to live to make changes. I know I've been changed.

I Must Tell Jesus All of My Problems; I Cannot Bear These Burdens Alone

Keisha Boone's Testimony

I didn't realize how empty my life was going to be without my son, Que, my first and only child. He must be coming around a lot. I can feel his presence. I thank God I met Jose. I don't know what or even if I would still be alive. Aunt Margaret is also a definite factor as to why I am still alive. I'm sitting here on the sofa now, watching TV with Jose. I have my drink and he has a drink while feeling relaxed, cool, and mellow. I can't believe just two years ago I was popping pills, drinking, and running after a so-called friend. I was going through a separation; I didn't have money for food but had money somehow for alcohol and money for my beautiful dog, Diamond. It was crazy getting drunk then popping pills, and now I'm here. I am calm, happy, and alive. Thank God!

I do realize without God I would have nothing. I often wondered why God has me here. It seems like I'm everyone's punching bag, or they use me for their mockery. I try and try, but it seems like nothing is working. Every job I have, it seems like the same situation happens. It starts off great, then something messes it up. I do know one thing that I am grateful for, and that is not being married. I hate marriage. I am thankful for my home, my life, and thankful to God that he has let me see another day.

God! Sitting here after taking a bath, after sitting there for two hours. Every time I let someone in my life or let someone get close to me, I always get hurt. That's why I choose to stay to myself. In 2021 I will try my hardest to focus more on nothing but God and getting out of Virginia.

I Surrender All

Harvey's Response

I belong to a twelve-step fellowship in which I'm not allowed to use their name but contribute its principles to my recovery. Their principles are based on a twelve-step modulus. I had to acquire the principle that I live to learn and I learn to live. One day I came to the realization that alcohol was more destructive to me than the drugs I was using because it was less expensive and easier to access. I used to drink beer as most people drink coffee in the morning. Some people do not consider alcohol as a drug, but it is a drug. Alcohol is a mind-altering substance. It tends to ease the pains and provide a fun-like pleasure that's hard to resist once you retain a taste for it. I had so many blackouts and loss of memory. I had to depend on people to tell me what I did the night before because I couldn't remember anything.

One time I was arrested for robbery. I woke up in a jail cell and had to be told that I was arrested on a felony charge. Not me! I would never rob anyone. When I went to the interrogation room, the detective asked me who was with me when I robbed Be-Lo's grocery store. I replied that they had me mixed up, I did not rob a store. I was drunk, but I knew I wouldn't have done anything like robbing a store. Then the detective showed me a picture and asked, "Is that you?" Much to my surprise, it was me looking at the camera—smiling! I had hit rock-bottom and stopped destroying myself. Once again, I proclaimed God had his hands on me, and he answered invested prayers.

Love Lifted Me

Margaret's Response

My alcohol habit was only moderate. I would join fellow teachers on Fridays after work and hang out at a local bar or restaurant, serving drinks. A few laughs, singing, and storytelling exchanges seemed so harmless, but eventually I realized I was supposed to be a new creature in Christ, as revealed in 2 Corinthians 5:17. When I did my self-examinations, I discovered that I had a people-pleasing addiction. It was more important that I meet my so-called friends' expectations over aligning my decisions and reactions with the Word of God. Deeper self-examination convinced me that I was wearing a mask on Sundays at church. I had to look in the mirror. Looking beyond my exterior, I found an inferiority complex within my soul. God help me. I was doubled-minded, a hypocrite! I had to stop compromising and rationalizing and put my Bible reading into obedience, my prayers into sincerity and stronger beliefs. I had to stop thinking and saying negative things about myself as well as others. I had to stop gossiping. I had to stop judging people and placing my misguided expectations on people. I truly love everybody, but I had to start loving myself. I asked God for forgiveness, but I had trouble forgiving myself. When I did, I had reached the spiritual level pursuing sanctification so I can truly be a new creature in Christ.

I Will Never Forget What He Has Done for Me

Tony Kensler

My name's Tony. I'm thirty-nine years old—just recently turned thirty-nine on February 28. Today is March 8th, about ten days from my birthday. Lessons, man. Invested blessing or invested prayers is what my aunt, Mrs. Margaret Mears, wanted me to speak on and share with y'all. I don't even know where to start. Things I'm thankful for that God put into my life is…first of all, first and foremost, the family that I have, the family that I was born into, the bloodline that I have is awesome. Like my family's support—I love my family. They're all unique in their own way. Personally, just to get more personal, I've been through a lot in my life. In and out of trouble. I've done the juvenile system, I've been in the adult prison system, maximum…you know, just being reckless. I can say this: one thing about me is, even through all the trouble and drama and traumatic things I've been through in my life, I've always had a good side, a good heart, I've always known that God is in my life. I've never been evil, plain evil, or done evil things. That's why the things that I've done, the things that I've been through, I've always been able to bounce back from.

I've been shot—I have six bullet holes in my body. I've shot people. You know, not to go into detail about it, but I've done things I regret too. And that's just a part of karma, just a part of life sometimes. I've been in car accidents and have scars all over my body. I've been through a lot in my life, a lot of traumatic things. But one thing

I'm grateful for is, even though I've hit my head a lot of times, I'm still able to breathe and have the opportunity to get my life together. Now I've got a beautiful family, I'm waiting to have a beautiful child of my own, but in the meantime, I have a beautiful baby girl. She's not my biological child, but I care for her like she's my daughter. That's one of the blessings in my life. You know, I've prayed for this.

Unfortunately, I lost my mother in the middle of my prison sentence in 2012, on January 23, 2012. I lost my mother, and she was the most precious person to me. All she wanted was to see me come home and succeed to the potential that she knew I had. I've always had potential, I've always been intelligent, but sometimes I just have problems with being influenced. I wouldn't say I've been a follower because I've always made my own ways and set my own footprints, but at the same time, there were certain influential peers I'd been around who got me into situations and trouble where I ended up having to call my mother. She was always there for me, that's one thing about her. She was always there.

It may be a blessing in disguise. The loss I had to take may be the reason I changed my life and started thinking smarter for my family. At the end of the day, it's not about me. It's about the people who love me. I'm blessed for that. Right now, I have a career. I was working a job before but figured I needed more for my family, so I went and got my CDL license. Right now, I have a job where I make $24 an hour, great benefits. I also work at dealerships part-time. So I have two jobs currently. I'm also looking into this business venture of owning a corner store in my neighborhood, possibly. There's so many things to be grateful for that I'll continue to appreciate. I'm happy to still be breathing, and I really just wanna make my family happy. I want them to be proud of me. I'm here for a reason, I know I am. I think I've already figured it out. I know my purpose, and that's what every man needs to figure out. What's your purpose? Everyone has one out here. If you're still here, still living, still breathing, it's for a reason. God got you here for a purpose, so figure that out and pursue it.

Investing in prayers is actually what keeps me motivated and knowing I can do anything. If I could come home from fourteen years of prison and make money that dudes who've never even been to prison are making, that shows a lot. That shows that anybody could do it. I've got that CDL with all the endorsements—tanker, triples and doubles, hazmat. I've got access to the Virginia international gateway, things like that. Anything is possible, and I'm a felon! If you just want to get your life together, it can happen. You've gotta want it. I wanted it. This was on my mind; I used to pace my cell in solitary confinement thinking about what I want to do, over and over. I used to ask myself, "What do I wanna do when I get out? I'm going to do this, I'm going to do that." I came out, and I did it. I exceeded expectations, and this is only the beginning. Invested prayers.

He Saw the Best in Me

Margaret's Response

I can literally shout for Tony's testimony because I have witnessed the manifestations of the many prayers I invested for him. Thank you, Jesus. I recall visiting the prison for his graduation. My sister was in hospice care. She tried with all her might to hold on until Tony was released from prison. She departed earth hearing me promising to look out for her children. Once again, I am acting as a mother.

As a teacher in special education, there were many occasions I found myself in the role of a mother. I was assigned to a class in Queens Hospital. I had to advise, teach, and comfort students with serious emotional problems. A sixteen-year-old female was involved with a traumatic experience. She had to witness her foster mother shooting her foster father, and then assist in dragging his body to their backyard. She even helped her mother dig a grave for him. There were several stories coming from young teenage girls who had been sexually assaulted by a family member. The boys' stories and conditions were breaking the law; they were either gang-related or had to do with confusion of gender identity. Most of the situations were very, very challenging, and we had not been professionally trained with effective skills warranting success. I resolved I needed Jesus. I invested many prayers daily for these students.

I know that above my college training, Christ is the answer to every difficult challenge. I had to demonstrate unconditional love to my children, my students, my friends, and anyone who crosses my path. My journey became less burdensome when I realized I only have God to please. People have too many expectations for me. I can't please everybody! I can find the answers to all my problems in my Bible. My successes, my retirement, and my marriage are results of God seeing the best in me.

Hold On to God's Unchanging Hand

Harvey's Response

My mind went back to a day in drug court when I was instructed to sit in the middle of a circle, surrounded with twelve drug addicts and the clinicians. I had to tell my story. I had to reveal what made me start drugs. I had to acknowledge all of my resentments. When I start talking, I start to cry. I had seen my father beat my mother for no reason. I recalled him being so jealous of my mother once when he woke up in an alcoholic stupor and fired his pistol at a coat that was hanging on a pipe. He thought it was a man! I expressed my gratitude for my grandmother but needed to express unfair whippings I received. I was so disappointed when my mother's siblings seemed to have abandoned us. We never heard from them. I believe my father's family was aware of the beatings my mother took from my father, but no one tried to stop him. I explained how I felt being called names pertaining to my head. I recalled the many women who cheated on me, even Cynthia, whom I lived with as a common-law husband for twenty years or more, cheated on me. I was hurt to recognize the lack of visitations or correspondence from my siblings when I was in prison. I felt abandoned during the times I was left uncared for and unattended to after my surgeries. I had so much to say, but I didn't use any of these resentments as an excuse for drug use. I was just plagued by these things that made me angry, and I tried to ease the internal battles that caused so much pain. These acknowledgments made me realize I didn't love myself at that point.

So I took on the challenges of doing things for myself, becoming independent. I did go to people I thought I had offended and asked for forgiveness. Some of those people had passed on in death.

After my surgeries, I did things for myself that the doctors told me I would not be able to do. They told me I wouldn't be able to work anymore, but now I take on odd jobs to fulfill the family budget by the grace of God. I rely on God more than ever before, and in this day and time, I continue to invest prayers.

Without God, I Can Do Nothing

Years ago, my Uncle June told me there were many relatives, neighbors, friends, and associates who predicted I would not see 30 years of age. Praise God, I doubled that number in September 2021. I am grateful to God for answering my grandmother's invested prayers.

I know I have changed. For 13 years, I haven't had any alcohol or used any alternating substances—not even medically prescribed substances for pain. I am truly grateful that I have no desire to live the lifestyle I used to live. I found the Lord in prison. I will always remember the visiting clergy that prayed for me after relentless abuse from fellow inmates. I backslid for 8 years, but I started making changes when I went to drug court.

God has answered my invested prayers. He has given me a God-loving wife. He has given me a church-worshipping family that has received me and encouraged me to be a better Christian. My anointed pastor, Reverend William J. Spencer, has excelled in reaching and teaching me to be a spiritual man.

I am convicted to align myself with biblical principles. I will bless the Lord at all times. People who get to know me realize I am real. I don't bite my tongue, but I must practice diligently thinking before I speak. Whatever one may think of my reflections, please believe it's God's grace and mercy that brought me this far. I want to live so God can use me.

Leaning and Depending on the Lord

The culminating statement pertaining to my reflections is that I learned from my mistakes. I sincerely regret the wrong thinking followed by sinful reactions. I have grown since those events. I have earnestly decided to let my little light shine. I have decided to spend more time reading and studying God's word. More importantly, I intend to obey his word more than ever before. All of my intentions are based on past failures, rebellious attitudes, procrastinating spirit, and ensuring I don't fall into those patterns again. I am praying for richer discernment with increasing and intentional praise.

I do not know what the future holds for me. I desire to continue living the best life I ever lived. I feel assured this marriage has a lasting strength because I've learned my past mistakes. My relationship with family and friends will not include people-pleasing. I have learned that negative thinking, judgemental thinking, and unrealistic expectations of people do more harm than good. I have endeavored to mind my own business, to spend more time and energy witnessing for the Lord by developing a stronger and more sincere relationship with Him.

My plans are to invest more in prayers for our nation, political leaders, community, and the health and wellbeing of people everywhere. I want to be real and sincere in my service to people. I love people! I want to display the Fruit of the Spirit everyday of my life through practice and determination. I need to amend my relationship with my brother, Donald, and his family. I want the world to know just how much I love him. I'm pressing on.

Acknowledgements

Thank you for your testimony!

Reverend Kevin Blane
Keisha Boone
Berthina Burns
Carolyn Chester
Deacon Larry Cypress
Cynthia Ford
Barbara Gurley
Tony Kensler
Marion Kirby
Peggy Lawrence
Charlesetta McCollough
Joanne Moore
Helen Moore
Audrey Morton
Arnika Nichols

Jane Valentine

And thank you for your contributions to the editing process…

Trae Bailey
Cynthia Hudson
Cindy Phillips
Erica Webb
Sierra Webb (cover designer)

Nakia Witherspoon

About the Author

Margaret Ann Mears was born in Baltimore, Maryland, but spent much of her adolescence and adult life in New York. Working as a teacher in the past, Margaret has always dreamed of writing a book of her own. She wholeheartedly has faith in God, and hopes that such devotion shows through her work.

Harvey Mears was born and continues to reside in Newport News, Virginia, with his wife, Margaret. Despite having lost his way as a young teenager, he loves the Lord and is always willing to help those in need. He's contributing to this book in hopes of showing others what is possible when you trust in God.

Together, the Mearses are a compassionate and loving couple who have dedicated their lives to their Christian faith. They present to the reader their individual trials, hardships, and other experiences as a method of healing and growth, examining the testimony of friends, family, and colleagues as they relate to their own lives. The title of their book, *Invested Prayers*, was derived from their observations of daily devotions. When they testified about past events and problems, references were usually made that their grandparents, a pastor, and even themselves prayed. They called those prayers invested prayers.

CPSIA information can be obtained
at www.ICGtesting.com
Printed in the USA
BVHW061515020522
635572BV00002B/8